The Effective Architect

THE
EFFECTIVE
ARCHITECT

WENDELL E. ROSSMAN

PRENTICE-HALL, INC.   Englewood Cliffs, N. J.

Prentice-Hall International, Inc., London
Prentice-Hall of Australia, Pty. Ltd., Sydney
Prentice-Hall of Canada, Ltd., Toronto
Prentice-Hall of India Private Ltd., New Delhi
Prentice-Hall of Japan, Inc., Tokyo

© 1972 by
PRENTICE-HALL, INC.
Englewood Cliffs, N. J.

Library of Congress
Catalog Card Number: 77-168618

Printed in the United States of America
ISBN-0-13-240754-X
B & P

The Author

WENDELL E. ROSSMAN's experience extends into nearly every phase of architecture, not only because of the large repertoire of buildings he has to his name, but also through his continued studies (he holds a Doctorate in Engineering) and extensive travels.

A native of Munich, Bavaria, he came to the United States in the late 1950s, opened his own architectural office and within a few years had built a successful practice. His education in Switzerland and Canada, where he worked as an architectural draftsman, construction engineer and architect, was followed by a period with the Alberta government, as senior architect, where he was entrusted with many large projects of complex technical nature including acoustics.

At his firm, Rossman and Associates, Phoenix, Arizona, he presently devotes about one-third of his efforts to a combination of abstract and practical building research and to the development of method approaches and new concepts. The research is time-problem oriented and deals exhaustively with such subjects as airports, prefabricated buildings, thin shell structures, and others. His work has been publicized nationally and internationally, especially in the field of air terminals. Dr. Rossman is the originator of a continually increasing number of patents in the U.S. and abroad.

To my son,
Michael David

About This Book

Why is there only a small fraction of architects who have become so eminently successful, while the majority seems to do little better than hold their own? Architects' educations are, by and large, quite similar, their opportunities nearly equal, and offices are patterned much alike.

In the early years of my own practice, this awareness prompted me to analyze the general practice of architecture, not so much on the level of what kind of time card to use, or how the organizational pattern of my staff should be, or the graphic beauty of my firm's logo — all things important, of course, but it seemed to me only secondary.

My investigation centered on the *conditiones sine quae non* of the successful architect. How to obtain commissions, how to design to please, how to omit errors, and how to communicate with the client. The purpose of this book is to convert these intangibles into tangibles, to offer methods and systems which achieve mastery over these essentials.

This book is written for the broad majority of practicing architects with offices from one to thirty members and annual volumes from a few hundred thousand to twenty or more millions. It will be of greatest benefit to the practitioner who is in the mainstream of American building, whose office is engaged in the broad range of structures from small alteration projects to multimillion dollar complexes; who by perseverance, intelligence and professionalism must obtain his commission, meet budgets, deal with his clients and engineers, but whose accomplishments must nonetheless be on a higher plane.

The book should be of value to architects in training who have aspirations toward their own practice. Finally, it is hoped that educators in the field of architecture may find some substance in the methods and procedures which have had their origins in a successful practice.

One highlight of this book is the treatise on the relationship between good design and a successful office, both reduced to the realm of practical attainability. Another high point is methods of how to obtain commissions, from the isolation of the real projects to the final assault — the presentation of one's firm in an interview. Of importance, also, are ways to avoid and deal with the high bid. An entire chapter is devoted to this subject, with cost controls at the beginning, estimating, and what to do if bids run over. Case histories of post bid negotiations illuminate the most significant approaches.

The book also offers suggestions for avoiding errors or correcting them once they have occurred. Errors ranging from a detail that will not work, to a functional or design miscalculation, to major malfunctions are discussed, with the six cardinal rules for "the avoidance before the fall."

Three chapters in the book deal with the somewhat controversial subject of the architect's education, in particular after school, with a proposal of what should be learned, how, and why, and how the acquired knowledge can be traded almost immediately for profit dollars. Another often controversial area covered is publicity and advertising, and the book offers suggestions and proposals for the individual firm as well as the professional society.

The concern for excellence of operations in one's office is a very real one for the successful architect. This attitude, coupled with his awareness that good design is the key to professional success, should enable the reader to put the substance of this book to work in his daily efforts toward individual prestige and increased profits.

Wendell E. Rossman

Contents

The Effective Architect

chapter 1

Key to Professional Success: Good Design

THE STILL UNDISPUTED realm of the architect is the design of buildings. Eventually his success will rest upon this single ability: excellence of design.

Therefore, the effective architect must adopt design techniques which improve not only quality but also efficiency. He has the right to harvest the greatest share of profits from design. This he can do if he takes advantage of methods and systems approaches.

This chapter examines the attributes of the designer, followed by techniques and systems approaches of design. The latter is explained by an example of a nontypical building.

Good Design Marks the Professional

Good design is a single harmonious cast. It is without contradiction, shortcomings or significant compromise. Good design pleases at first sight and remains timelessly pleasant. It is that which eventually signifies the greatness of an architect.

When I speak of good design as the key to professional success, I place the emphasis on the word *professional*. In architecture, there cannot be material success (a desirable state) without preceding professional success (a satisfying state). The effective architect must, therefore, most arduously concern himself with the professional success.

It makes little difference to our fellowmen what else the architect does or doesn't do; he is judged, with anything from contempt to extravagant praise, by his creations, his designs. That, in the final analysis, is what will bring him more commissions, more profits.

Failing of the Common Approach

Significantly enough, design must emerge in a single act to be good. The common trial and error, or pencil roulette, approach is not only inefficient, but never results in good design. To be sure, the over-abundance of new materials, the constant emergence of yet more design fashions and modes are like a multi-page menu — a choice from which is quite difficult. If there were many, many solutions one could use, design would be a process of selecting from the horn of plenty. Nothing could be further from the case.

Good design is an optimum solution. The choice is not between possibilities but between components, materials and arrangements so they may be placed into harmonious conjugation, as all larger systems must be made up of smaller elements, elements which are ordered within themselves.

Talent or Hard Work?

To many architects the attribute "design ability" is a bit elusive and sometimes slightly discouraging. It is generally believed to be a question of talent, but can good design only be the product of the gifted few? True, there are minds who possess a greater ability to visualize spatial relationships, and who with an apparent magic touch can create beauty. But most often the talented designer treats the surface and not the spaces. Design has many facets: that of the spaces to enclose the activity, the relationship of these spaces to each other, the structural frame, the characteristics of the material and lastly the surface configuration. All of these facets must be brought into concordance to achieve good design. Often ignored until ten minutes before the bid opening, there is also the budget.

Before I deal with the techniques of efficient and successful design, I should like to speak about creativity — or, the ability to transmute matter into a higher order, an ability whose foundations are professional skill, discipline and taste. What I do not mean is the deftness of the stylist with his momentarily charming, but utterly substance-less designs. Now then, how much of creativity is truly a gift of God and how much is personal achievement?

Taste

The attribute of taste is the ability to distinguish between good and bad, good and better, logical or inconsistent, befitting or out of place, pleasing or uninspiring — in short to recognize the scales and nuances of values and select those necessary for a tasteful decision. While one mind may be better equipped to perform this task, it is nevertheless something which can be acquired by learning.

Discipline

The matter of discipline is of somewhat different nature. Firstly, a spiritual accomplishment, it is the result of self-education, self-denial and an endeavor to conquer the higher levels of one's mind. There is no royal road to discipline, not even a ready-made approach. Yet, it is precisely the virtue which in architecture has brought accomplishments to the most lofty status! Discipline in architecture is to a great extent the voluntary submission to self-imposed rule, be that rule empirically proven good or be it newly set down for a given structure.

A good analogy is composition within the rules of harmonic music. If the basic interval of the octave is altered by even the most minute quantity, the sound becomes exceedingly ugly since it is out of tune. Likewise, other intervals such as the third, the fifth and even the tierce must submit to precise mathematical relationships lest they sound discordant. But not only must the intervals be correct, sequence of pitch and time of a melody are to follow a definite rule to express a thought or feeling. Two or more melodies simultaneously, respecting the empirical "contrapuntal law," form a complex sound pattern. The composer's creation lies entirely within the self-imposed rule, that is, recognized laws of harmony, and is therefore timelessly beautiful. This kind of discipline can indeed be learned.

Professional Skill: Mastery Through Practice

It represents the self-constructed road through knowledge, a road along which one can travel swiftly and unerringly. Professional skill in architecture is the knowledge of almost countless technical, artistic, economical, sociologic and historical pieces of information and data. To know where to find it is, at least by the process of designing, inadequate. Again, a high measure of knowledge can be acquired without the necessity of a special talent.

The Gift of God

Nevertheless, there is an element which cannot be learned: imagination. For this characteristic there is no substitute. Yet imagination by itself would be ineffectual. Its effect would be momentary, like pyrotechnics. In architecture, imagination can only produce lasting advances if it is combined with taste, discipline and professional skill. But while the one in a million who has all these attributes may determine a new direction and set the pace, the million who possess all but imagination will build the road to follow.

Daring

There is one point I want to make before leaving this subject. Highly disturbing to all complacent men, another ingredient is one mentioned only after the act: daring. Daring is the vehicle of imagination. Without it new thoughts will not materialize. The world and society per se is made up of conservatives; as their material status becomes more and more comfortable, the concept of daring becomes more frightening to them.

Throughout my professional life I have found this behavior the most discouraging aspect of my existence. Architects who have "made it" are also guilty of cowardice; their comfortable status might be shaken by daring. In the broad picture, they will amount to no more than a cobblestone in the road—comfortable, secure and trodden upon.

The daring and the imaginative mind faces forever new walls of thorns through which he will be driven by inner conviction. While his lot is difficult and thankless, he may nevertheless claim the breakthrough into the unknown and the initiation of a new direction.

I cannot encourage my fellow architects enough to exhibit daring, to propose new ideas fearlessly. The stature of the architect will not suffer. A loss of commissions, if it does occur, is infinitesimal. But the stakes are high enough to make the small risks worthwhile. If nothing else, it will shake the infuriatingly complacent brain-cages of our fellowmen.

Techniques of Design

The fee structure for architectural work permits little or no leeway at all, demanding therefore highly efficient systems, techniques and approaches to the practical performance. One of the most neglected areas is techniques of design. An office may have a so-called good designer but invariably his pretty pictures are taken from him at a certain stage and handed to a trusted, well-experienced team captain who, with the obligatory air of contempt towards the dreamer, then translates some of the designs into practical and constructible entities.

A good designer who has the ability of immediate translation into the practical and, to go one step further, the skill and the imagination to determine the most elegant structural frame, is likely to be found only in very small offices. Since he will not yield his prerogatives to anyone else, he can only design and process so many dollars of buildings in a given time.

These very common approaches are compromises with severe limitations. One isn't really architecture and the resulting work is uniform, inoffensive and totally uninspiring. The other method does indeed produce architecture of the highest order. But the fees which are generally paid make the method not only unlucrative but a constant gamble with one's professional existence.

Most architects have experienced the gnawing feeling of uncertainty about the true position of their designs within the scale of the conceivable, a scale ranging from the mediocre to the brilliant optimum. It is this very uncertainty which leads to the inefficient and frustrating tries for alternative solutions. How many an architect has gone the full circle, through seemingly endless sketches of different approaches in both plan and facade, to return eventually to his first design! He is now where he started, none the wiser but perhaps a bit more relieved: he has tested his design and "proven" it to be the best. The process was neither time or money saving, nor is proof by one's own testing so irrefutable that one is put fully at ease.

This undesirable situation is largely due to a common haphazard approach which treats design as an artistic composition, with the aid of lots of graphics: colorful circles, arrows, coded lines and boundaries, all on stacks of transparent paper. Thus, the lion's share of the design fee is used up. The one opportunity the architect has to make a good profit has been missed.

While it is a matter of internal organization and staff-casting to determine the person and degree of work to be performed, the subsequent topics will concern themselves with a design technique.

I have over the years developed a system which has greatly increased the quality of my designs and simultaneously shortened the design time dramatically.

The system prevents most errors or excessive compromises, yet permits an extremely rapid succession of steps of refining and ordering. Most of all, any random grouping or pencil roulette is eliminated. I have many times managed to design structures ranging in cost from one-half to several million dollars in a matter of two to three weeks, so complete and logical that virtually no major changes were made to the day when construction was complete.

My profits rose immediately. The system eventually produced design data which equalled contract documents of other architects, yet rarely does the cost exceed 0.75% of the building value. The technique clearly separates all that which can be routine from the pure creative act.

The most important tool is notation. Analogous to mathematics, concise notation of a building program is half the solution: it presents the problem in orderly fashion, suggesting function linkage and space arrangements and, of course, minimizes errors.

A building program is like a 3-dimensional equation with a multitude of complex terms (components) and functions. The optimum solution is the most desirable assemblage of all components as a 3-dimensional configuration, and the best possible inter-linkage of the various functions. To satisfy all the human activities, there is an almost infinite number of possible programs. The program may vary from a single room to a complex mega-structure.

Notation

The first step to obtain an overall view of the program is simple listing and indexing. The initial listing of rooms may be at random. At this point, it is unnecessary to recognize grouping at all. Once all rooms or facilities have been listed, grouping is undertaken by attaching numbers to functions and decimals to facilities or rooms in descending order of physical size and/or significance.

In the following example, I have chosen a civic auditorium program for music, theater and conventions. The house is to seat 3200 with divisibility into four spaces: of 800 (little theater); 400 and 400 (meeting and recital rooms); and 1600 (permanent).

Let it be assumed that the following major rooms are the substance of the program:

Facility	Function.Facility	Facility	Function.Facility
Main Hall, seating 3200	1.0	First Aid Room	2.7
Little Theater, seating 800	1.1	4 Practice Rooms	4.41
Stage	3.0	Male Dressing Room	4.0
Orchestra Pit	3.2	Female Dressing Room	4.1
Foyer	2.0	Star Cubicles	4.2
Ticket Booth	2.3	Green Room	4.6
Exhibit. Room	2.5	Costume Sewing	4.3
Exhibit. Room	2.6	Costume Designing	4.31
Public Toilets	2.1	Rehearsal Room	4.4
Cloak Rooms	2.2	Stage Shop	3.3
Concessions	2.4	Paint Shop	3.4
Forestage	3.1	Mus. Dressing Room (Male)	5.0
Light Control Booth	3.8	Mus. Dressing Room (Female)	5.1
Sound Control Booth	3.7	Conductor's Suite	5.3
Janitors	6.3	Musician's Library	5.2
Central Supply Room	6.2	Instrument Room	5.4
Quick-Change Room	4.5	Trap Room	3.6
General Storage	6.1	Actor's Lounge	4.7
Mechanical Room	6.0	Director's Suite	4.8
Managerial Office	6.4	Recital Room, seating 400	1.2
Musician's Lounge	5.5	Meeting Room, seating 400	1.3
Little Theater, Dressing Room	1.11	Stage Design Studio	3.5
Little Theater, Stage Storage	1.12		

The numbers are attached to the rooms after the first listing, thus ordering the facilities according to function and also to determine basic interrelation within each function. 1.0 denotes the house; 1.1, 1.2 and 1.3, the divisible rooms; e.g., sub-features of the house. 2. is the characteristic of the foyer group with everything belonging to it. The 3. group denotes the stage and supporting rooms; 4., the actor's quarters; 5., the musicians, and services are in group 6.

The program is now rewritten in the new notation which orders functions and facilities:

1.   Main House   3200/1600

1.1	Little Theater 800
1.2	Recital Room 400
1.3	Meeting Room 400
1.11	Little Theater Stage
1.12	Little Theater Dr. Rms.
1.13	Little Theater Stage Stg.

2.   Foyer

2.1	Public Toilets
2.2	Cloak Rooms
2.3	Ticket Booth
2.4	Concessions
2.5	Exhibition Room
2.6	Exhibition Room
2.7	First Aid Room

3.   Stage

3.1	Forestage
3.2	Orchestra Pit
3.3	Stage Shop
3.4	Paint Shop
3.5	Designer's Studio
3.6	Trap Room
3.7	Sound Control Booth
3.8	Light Control Booth

4.   Actor's Quarters

4.0	Male Dressing Room
4.1	Female Dressing Room
4.2	Star Cubicles
4.3	Costume Sewing
4.31	Costume Designing
4.4	Rehearsal Room
4.41	Four Practice Rooms
4.5	Quick-Change Rooms
4.6	Green Room
4.7	Actor's Lounge
4.8	Director's Suite

5.   Musician's Quarters

5.0	Musician's Dr. Room (Male)
5.1	Musician's Dr. Room (Female)
5.2	Musician's Library
5.3	Conductor's Suite
5.4	Instrument Room
5.5	Musician's Lounge

6.   Services

6.0	Mechanical Rooms
6.1	General Storage
6.2	Central Supply Room
6.3	Janitors
6.4	Managerial Offices (or 2.31)

Introduction of the Budget

Since the majority of all buildings must fit into a budget, let it be assumed that this is also the case in the present example. It is, therefore, necessary to employ a sequence of priority in the distribution of quantities. The next notation, therefore, distinguishes between desired and mandatory.

Facility	*Desired* (sq. ft.)	*Mandatory* (sq. ft.)
1.0 House, including 1.1, 1.2, 1.3	30,000	30,000
1.11, 1.12, 1.13 (Little Theater)	2,500	1,500

Facility (continued)		*Desired* (sq. ft.)	*Mandatory* (sq. ft.)
2.0	Foyer	7,000	3,000
2.1	Public Toilets	400	400
2.2	Cloak Rooms	600	200
2.3	Ticket Booth	250	150
2.4	Concessions	400	100
2.5	Exhibition Room	3,000	
2.6	Exhibition Room	3,000	
2.7	First Aid Room	200	200
		47,350	35,550
3.0	Stage	9,000	7,000
3.1	Forestage	1,400	1,400
3.2	Orchestra Pit	1,500	1,500
3.3	Stage Shop	6,000	2,000
3.4	Paint Shop	3,000	
3.5	Designer's Studio	1,600	
3.6	Trap Room	700	
3.7	Sound Control Booth	300	150
3.8	Light Control Booth	200	150
		23,700	12,200
4.0	Actor's Dressing Room (Male)	700	500
4.1	Actor's Dressing Room (Female)	700	500
4.2	Star's Cubicles	500	200
4.3	Costume Sewing	200	
4.31	Costume Designing	200	
4.4	Rehearsal Room	3,000	2,000
4.41	Four Practice Rooms	400	200
4.5	Quick-Change Rooms	300	100
4.6	Green Room	300	200
4.7	Actor's Lounge	600	
4.8	Director's Suite	200	150
		7,100	3,850
5.0	Musician's Dressing Room (Male)	500	400
5.1	Musician's Dressing Room (Female)	500	400
5.2	Musician's Library	250	100
5.3	Conductor's Suite	250	150
5.4	Instrument Room	200	100
5.5	Musician's Lounge	600	600
		2,300	1,750

Facility (continued)	*Desired* (sq. ft.)	*Mandatory* (sq. ft.)
6.0 Mechanical Rooms	4,000	4,000
6.1 General Storage	2,000	1,000
6.2 Central Supply Room	1,200	500
6.3 Janitors	300	200
6.4 Managerial Offices	500	300
	8,000	6,000
Totals	88,450	59,350
25% for Structural, Corridors, etc.	22,112	14,837
	110,562	74,187

The priority notation has produced two things: an overall view of areas and a practical choice of sizes.

The next step relates to cost estimates. This requires some caution since quality decisions are made as soon as unit costs are applied. As a safeguard, volume should also be taken into consideration. As an example, if a cubic foot for this type of construction and desired quality would be $1.30, the house, having a height of about 60 feet from basement to roof, would cost $78.00 per square foot. A foyer with 24-foot height would cost $31.20, but due to special appointments, more likely $45.00. In other words, good judgment must be used. The following notation is, therefore, a first estimate of the costs of the desirable and also the mandatory. The example is, like the previous notation, very much condensed and should in actual practice be quite detailed.

Areas and Unit Cost	*Desired*	*Mandatory*
1.0 House @ $78.00/sq. ft. (30,000)	$2,340,000.	$2,340,000.
1.11, 1.12, 1.13 @ $40.00/sq. ft.	100,000.	60,000.
2.0 to 2.7 Foyer Group @ $40.00/sq. ft.	594,000.	162,000.
3.0 Stage @ $110.00/sq. ft.	990,000.	770,000.
3.1 to 3.8 Stage Rooms @ $35.00/sq. ft.	514,500.	182,000.
4.0 to 4.8 Actor's Quarters @ $30.00/sq. ft.	213,000.	115,500.
5.0 to 5.5 Musician's Quarters @ $30.00/sq. ft.	69,000.	52,500.
6.0 to 6.4 Services @ $20.00/sq. ft.	160,000.	120,000.
	$4,980,500.	$3,802,000.
Corridors, etc. @ $20.00	442,240.	296,740.
	$5,422,740.	$4,098,740.
Special Equipment	450,000.	220,000.
Site Work	600,000.	600,000.
	$6,472,740.	$4,918,740.

The foregoing demonstrated that the auditorium should cost $6,472,740., but could also be built for $4,918,740. Since a budget of $6,000,000. is applied to this example, the final notation, or the working program, must reflect area adjustments.

Working Program

Facility		Area	Height	Unit	Total
		Dimensions (ft.)		*Cost*	*($)*
1.0	House	30,000	40	78	2,340,000
1.1	Little Theater	incl.			
1.2	Meeting Room	incl.			
1.3	Recital Room	incl.			
1.11	Stage (Little Theater)	1,500	30	50	75,000
1.12	Stage Storage	300	15	30	9,000
1.13	Dressing Rms. (Little Theater)	200	10	30	6,000
2.0	Foyer	6,500	20	45	292,500
2.1	Public Toilets	400	10	50	20,000
2.2	Cloak Rooms	300	10	20	6,000
2.3	Ticket Booth	200	10	30	6,000
2.4	Concessions	400	10	40	16,000
2.5,2.6	Exhibition Rooms	2,500	20	35	87,500
2.7	First Aid Room	200	10	30	6,000
3.0	Stage	8,000	80	110	880,000
3.1	Forestage	1,400	40	80	112,000
3.2	Orchestra Pit	1,500	10	25	37,500
3.3	Stage Shop & Storage	4,000	35	50	200,000
3.4	Paint Shop	1,000	35	50	50,000
3.5	Studio and Layout	1,000	20	30	30,000
3.6	Trap Room	700	20	35	24,500
3.7,3.8	Control Suites	400	10	45	18,000
4.0	Actor's Dressing Room, Male	500	10	30	15,000
4.1	Actor's Dressing Room, Female	500	10	30	15,000
4.2	Star Cubicles	300	10	40	12,000
4.3,4.31	Costume Sewing & Designing	400	10	25	10,000
4.4	Rehearsal Room	2,500	24	40	100,000
4.41	2 Practice Rooms	200	10	25	5,000
4.5	Quick-Change Room	100	10	25	2,500
4.6	Green Room	300	12	45	13,500
4.7	Actor's Lounge	400	12	35	14,000
4.8	Director's Suite	200	12	30	6,000
5.0	Musician's Dr. Rm., Male	400	12	30	12,000
5.1	Musician's Dr. Rm., Female	400	12	30	12,000

| Facility (continued) | Dimensions (ft.) | | Cost | ($) |
	Area	Height	Unit	Total
5.2 Musician's Library	250	10	30	7,500
5.3 Conductor's Suite	150	10	35	5,250
5.4 Instrument Room	200	12	50	10,000
5.5 Musician's Lounge	400	12	30	12,000
6.0 Mechanical Rooms	4,000	14	20	80,000
6.1 General Storage	2,000	14	20	40,000
6.2 Central Supply	1,000	12	25	25,000
6.3 Janitors	200	10	25	5,000
6.4 Managerial Offices	400	12	30	12,000
	75,300			4,629,750
Corridors, etc. (25%)	18,825		20	376,500
Special Equipment & Site Work				1,000,000
	94,125			6,006,250

The working program should be compiled in as great detail as possible since it will serve as the backbone of the entire design process, as well as for economics, rentals and leases, staffing, operational cost and many others. The program must be accompanied by an operational analysis, for example, how the individual facilities, groups and clusters will be used. The analysis should again be most thorough. For example, the kinds of exhibits should be listed. Can the foyer be used as an exhibit hall? Does the auditorium separate into areas of use: exhibition rooms plus foyer plus concessions; and simultaneously little theater and meeting/recital rooms; and auditorium as an independent theater, also simultaneously? Can actor's and musician's lounges be used jointly? Should the managerial offices be in the front or stage area? Of course, every conceivable function on stage must be treated elaborately.

Graphic Analysis

A complete operational analysis is essential to proceed with the interrelation of functions and facilities — first within each group and then between entire groups. The working program, which has already been arranged so that groups can be manipulated separately, is thus transposed into the first step of a plan. The sequence of transposition is unimportant; one can begin with group or facility relationships. In the present example, facilities relationship is resolved first. By proceeding in this manner, group relationship usually becomes self-evident.

The design system considers the most important room and relates everything else to it. This space is represented by a single line. A line permits an abstract study of room relationships, something the usual circle does not. In fact, the circle forces one into peripheral grouping instead of solving relationships first, as one begins with a plan layout without first having established the matrix. The method is then a trial and error system.

In the example (Figure 1.1), the line is the house or auditorium and related to it are the rooms of groups 1 and 2. The reader should note that rooms are represented by squares which are in proper scale and size relationship to each other. The relationship of function is indicated by a double arrow. The arrow is coded graphically to indicate the magnitude of interrelationship, such as the number of people circulating between the two spaces or the movement of goods, in this case stage sets and materials.

The room relation diagram (1.1) serves also as a very useful tool in communication with the client. Before one proceeds with the next step, the graphic assembly, the client's approval can be obtained. The diagram can be understood by any reasonably intelligent lay person.

The next step is to take the house as related to the performer's side and in Figure 1.2, groups 3, 4 and 5 are related to the stage and also outside.

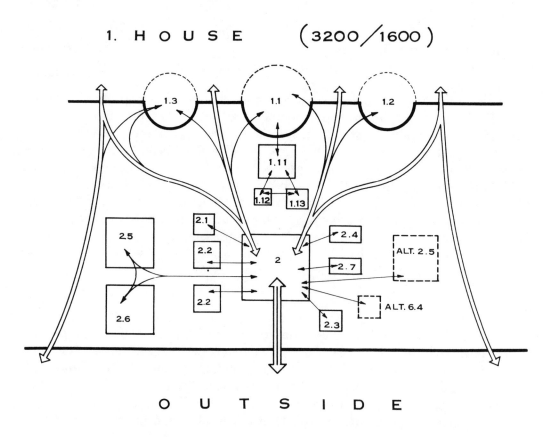

Fig. 1.1 Room Relation Diagram: Patrons. The diagram relates rooms between the house and the outside. Rooms are represented by squares of equal scale, double arrows as function relationships. Later on, the double arrows become the connecting corridors. The program of divisibility is solved by employing the TDA (turntable divisible auditorium) principle, where, through rotation of seating areas, double use is accomplished.

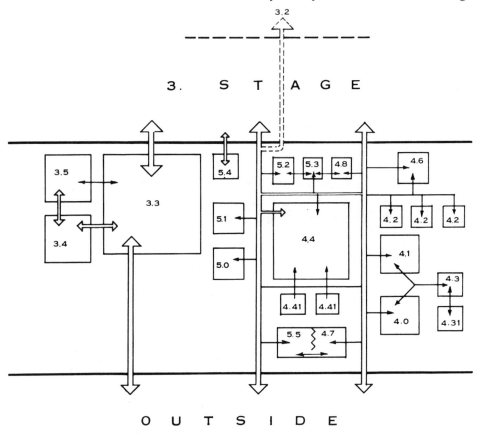

Fig. 1.2 Room Relation Diagram: Performers. The diagram is the simple transposition of previous data: the working program of kind, number and size of rooms, and the function pattern which related activities to the rooms and groups of rooms. A relationship diagram orders all factors graphically, as the first step in the actual planning.

Graphic Assembly

Up to the point of completing group relationship diagrams, the designer has been forced to follow a defined sequence of steps which, by virtue of the rule, yielded basic schematics as a potential optimum solution. Minor variations are obviously possible in the interpretation of interrelationship and may well be introduced in the final step. But these variations do not alter the potential optimum solution which resulted from the systematically formulated matrix established previously.

It is inevitable that a relationship diagram or graphic functions analysis preconditions the mind to a geometric arrangement. Any effort to disrelate it, such as saying "it only illustrates function," is psychologically strained. The design system specifically suggests an actual plan, intentionally relating sizes and traffic pattern.

The transposition into the first schematics is now relatively easy and the previously discussed attributes of taste, discipline, professional skill will become the tools which determine shape, vertical dimension and the formulation of spaces. This step may be spread out into two or more sub-steps, depending on the complexity of the project. In the example used here, one intermediate step, that of the group relation diagram (Fig. 1.3) illustrates the desirability of intermediate steps.

The group relation diagram has already circumscribed the principal coordinates of the new building's geometry. I have omitted the obvious steps of vertical relationships which are again diagrammatic line systems along arbitrarily chosen sections: through the axis, through stage, foyer, little theater and so on.

The final step in the design systems is the coordination of the group into a tangible plan. The step again is a short one since all support work has prepared the path. Fig. 1.4 illustrates the result of the step. From this point on, each group can be treated in detail by conventional planning methods.

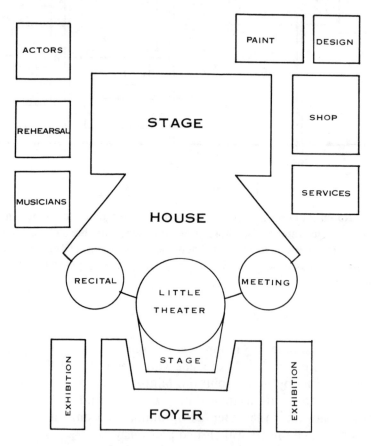

Fig. 1.3 Group Relation Diagram. Previously established diagrams are now interrelated to describe the entire building as it must function. At this point, the single line rooms have closed and should assume the general geometry. Also, these rooms (house and stage in the example) must be shown in proper scale relationship. The group relation diagram primarily relates groups but also recognizes the most significant rooms within each group.

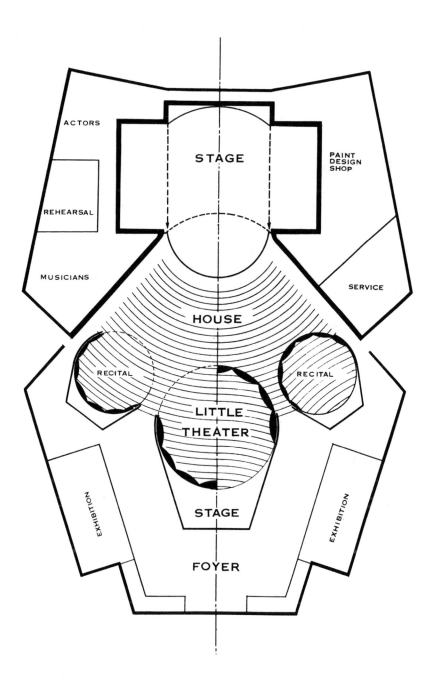

Fig. 1.4 Group Relation Plan. The groups are now ordered into a cohesive system: the schematic plan. Immediately following, the vertical space relationship is established — and, as a final step, the structural system. Beyond, only detail work is left.

The Structural System

With the existence of a schematic plan and all basic vertical coordinates, the structural system must be determined. Most architects wait all too long and leave the decision to the last. Others leave it to the engineer. Without it, it becomes a discoordinate heap of variably sized cubicles. It is beyond the scope of this book to discuss structural systems, regardless of how tempting to the writer. It is paramount in the orderly design sequence that upon arrival of a schematic plan all other work cease until the structure has been formulated. The consequence of negligence is backtracking or chaos, both costly.

Definition of a Design

Quite frequently during the presentation of the design the client may ask why this or that had been done in the plans. It seems that the architect usually lacks the answer — not because there was no good reason, but because he can't remember. In fact, the design of almost any building has so many ramifications that it may well be impossible to remember why, for example, this room is as shown.

Yet the client will demand his answer. If he does not get it, the architect is faced with the drudgery of backtracking until he has found the reason, or may, like it or not, have to change his design.

The notation and relation diagrams provide the ultimate memory banks because all steps are laid bare, ready for instantaneous re-inspection and proof. The defense of a design thus becomes a delightful task, an opportunity to impress the client.

chapter 2

The Way to Large Projects

A VAST SEGMENT of architecture must deal with the less interesting – additions, alterations, remodeling, a bit of face-lifting, and such things as parking lots and trash bins. To the effective architect these seemingly profitless and unalluring objects are, for several reasons, of keen interest. Properly approached and executed, they become the most reliable stepping-stones to bigger projects and a steadier flow of work.

This chapter illuminates the major areas from which such projects come and the methods and strategies for their successful execution. It concludes with a discussion of common favors expected from architects and the effects of one's response.

Omnium-Gatherum Constructionae

Mankind is in need of more than new buildings; the variety of functions, desires, habits, tradition, trends and fashions call for all kinds of alterations and a colorful array of structures of utilitarian and decorative nature. These may range from a planter box to a zoo pool for kodiaks, the remodeling of an old movie theater into a furniture store, or the design of a transformer station enclosure or carport addition – a grand variety which I will call, for lack of a better name, "omnium-gatherum constructionae."

Typical in this category is the slow process of completing a program through the successive additions of more and more omnium-gatherum. Some buildings are like a suit in a thrift shop: they must be altered to fit the newest owner. Yet other structures have become dated and must be whipped into more competitive — pardon me — contemporary shape, a process aptly called face-lifting and redecorating.

As a special segment of architecture, omnium-gatherum is difficult and complex. Who has not spent hours looking for a solution of how to support the superstructure at the junction of new and old, or how to hide, or better yet integrate, existing columns into a new plan or facade? Or how to overcome a chaos of floor elevations which make a new stair tower a Chinese puzzle of steps and landings! Or the often nightmarish foundation problems adjacent to old work! The annoyance of inadequate as-builts or field measured drawings — unexplorable floor systems, absolute mysteries of how the old contraption ever stood up!

Then the endless frustrations over the design of some silly thing like a 12-foot wide store front for an owner who wants a collection of materials from Roman brick through corrugated glass, marble, stainless steel to Venetian tile — the kind of problem with no apparent solution but 64 possibilities. And then the family room addition for the executive's house where he graciously (and slyly) lets his wife make the "aesthetic decisions," where one could turn out a 10,000 square foot warehouse faster than the fireplace design alone.

"Omnium-gatherum constructionae" makes no one's mouth water or mind elate, neither architects nor owners and I believe not even contractors.

The owner's dislike stems from his instinctive anticipation that what must be done will be expensive and difficult; first the dawning awareness that the architect will have to be consulted after all, that his fee is likely to be quite high, that his participation will waken a pack of sleeping dogs such as (un)necessary plans, building permits, contractors, inspectors, and, even though the results are better to be sure, it has cost far more than planned, budgeted, or necessary. What irks him most is that he knew all along that this is how it would turn out.

The architect on the other hand has no great enthusiasm either. He, too, knows instinctively that several risks are involved; he is likely to lose money because the work turns into more than he anticipated and his fee is therefore inadequate. He also views with joyless eyes the technical difficulties. Deep down, however, he simply resents what he is doing. His colleagues work on brand new, shining, million-dollar buildings, whereas he, the left-behind, must feed on the scraps. As a final insult, he is expected to work a miracle of low cost on the project.

The contractor, as the third party, approaches the omnium-gatherum with extreme caution. In particular, any work where he will have to break into existing construction bears the potential danger of becoming a bottomless pit into which to sink his money. To be sure, he has such devices as cost-plus contracts, but he is likely to face an irritated owner who may suddenly lose patience.

Omnium-gatherum is indeed a highly specialized area of architecture. It calls for ingenuity, intuition, a wealth of experience of types of constructions, a precise feeling for strengths of materials, plenty of aesthetics and a certain virtuosity in the preparation of drawings. Furthermore, the architect should be skilled personally in at least one of the key crafts to have a more natural approach to workable solutions for difficult details. In short, he who is capable of carrying through an omnium-gatherum project is a master of his profession.

The Stepping-Stone to Larger Projects

Although omnium-gatherum constructionae is not an obvious field in which to become wealthy, or have a pleasant and glamorous professional life, the effective architect nevertheless views the issue with detachment and soon finds most disadvantages, differently approached, turn into advantages.

First, it is usually the key to large projects, in particular when big, multi-building owners are involved. Secondly, referrals through one-time-only owners lead to other and usually larger commissions. Thirdly, it greatly aids the dissemination of one's good name.

I was asked once to design an orchestra shell for a symphony association, to improve the sound in an old school auditorium in which the symphony was accustomed to play. The shell performed well and was of reasonable appearance. Soon I received a plea from another symphony group to design one for their place of performance – an old movie theater-like hall. The problem was far more difficult and only marginal improvements were achieved. Nevertheless, the people were very pleased with the results, so much in fact that I decided to donate my time. Several years later, one of the directors of the symphony association embarked upon a building program. While other architects were on the spot, post haste, the director asked me to do the design.

The One-Time Owner

A client may be a one-time owner, never to build again, but as a person with estate and voice in a community, his opinion of the architect's performance is important to the professional; it enhances or degrades his image. Furthermore, persons who build, even if they only dabble in construction, meet with their own kind. Referrals therefore are particularly common.

The first step for the architect is that he must change his client's basic attitude. He must supplant the aura of suspicion and irritation with one of enthusiasm and confidence, with which the owner should look forward to his project. Not only will it make the task an easier one, but most important, one can thus obtain an adequate fee. The most effective method to dispel the client's suspicion is to proceed in the following manner:

1. A cursory survey of the project must be made. It is advisable to make it clear to the client that he is, at this point, under no obligation. No fees, ideas or cost should be discussed either. Experience has shown that most projects are feasible. However, alternative approaches would often be more desirable, be it for functional or economic reasons. It is quite simply a matter of professional skill to make that judgment after only the briefest of investigations. It would be neither useful nor ethical to engage in discussions about alternatives. At this point it is simply a matter of basic feasibility.

2. If the project is feasible and has merit, the prospective client should be so informed. Also, he must be told at this point that definite programs, costs, and the like, can only be determined through a thorough analysis. Since the analysis involves considerable work, an agreement must be reached first. It is advisable and acceptable to most clients to propose a two-step arrangement whereby the analysis will cost a certain fixed amount, or percentage of an estimated cost, and the actual work — design, construction documents and supervision — be a secondary sum.

3. Then follows a thorough analysis of the project. Technical aspects, construction cost, one's fee and the amount of unforeseeable matter must be investigated and discussed with the client. Even if the project is small, a written report is advisable. It also justifies beyond any doubt the cost of the initial analysis.

4. If the client's decision is to proceed, it is of great importance that he be kept informed of problems, their solution and a current cost picture. Nothing is more irritating to a client than surprises or the sudden presentation of a *fait accompli*.

It should be clear to architects that this client, if dealt with candidly from the beginning, will have no real objections to a just fee. The fees quite generally are higher than for a new building, but projects are so different that individual estimates of time versus construction cost should be made.

It is paramount that the division of fees into architecture and engineering, and the reason for the percentage or amount be explained to the client. This will greatly strengthen his confidence in the architect.

In summary, one should approach the omnium-gatherum project as a specialty, prepare exact proposals in stages and at all times maintain complete understanding with the client. Thus the work itself becomes interesting, adequately remunerated and inevitably leads to other and usually larger projects.

The Multi-Structure Client

Although the scope of the projects, technically as well as to kind, is similar when undertaken by large, repetitive clients like institutions, commercial or industrial concerns, the attitudes of such clients are different. Therefore, the architect must not only modify his approach but also his ultimate aim.

To the repetitive builder, omnium-gatherum is a common occurrence. He is emotionally quite uninvolved: to him these are projects of necessity and expediency. For these reasons he is neither greatly concerned over, nor disturbed by the cost involved. He is also well experienced, sometimes more so than the architect, as to what he is getting himself involved in. Such matters as fees are established issues to him. One thing, however, is often lacking: a cohesive master plan in which the omnium-gatherum is part of an ultimate target.

Because the absence of a master plan is quite common, the architect new to the plant should, as a matter of professional habit, make a general examination of the past pattern and future potential. If it is found that a master plan is indeed lacking and a thorough review is advisable, the architect should bring this to the attention of the owner.

In particular, educational institutions seem frequently to be devoid of any planning beyond the initial stage. Additions to these plants without masterplanning cause great inefficiency to the user and also wastefulness of land. The chances are better than even that an owner, to whom the concepts of masterplanning are made known, will request at least a restudy if not complete masterplanning procedure. I can point to many good-sized projects for which I was commissioned because I suggested a masterplanning based on a preliminary review.

As for the project in detail, this client knows what he wants. The architect need not concern himself with much analysis. The program is usually spelled out well, the solutions calling primarily for precise and thorough work. There are, however, two very significant points the architect must be aware of. The repetitive client is primarily a builder of large and often new structures, and the omnium-gatherum is more or less incidental. Therefore, he views the architect either from the viewpoint of (a) what potential he may have for large or new buildings or, (b) if he is engaged in large buildings on a steady basis, that the taking care of his omnium-gatherum is considered as a natural and expected favor in return.

Small Jobs Lead to Big Work

While still employed by others, I was baffled yet impressed by the devotion and painstaking care with which my boss treated certain small projects. While I was not always wholly convinced that the motive was to create architectural beauty, the results in that area were nevertheless quite acceptable. But much more impressive were the after-effects.

Not far from the office stood an old, sprawling, discoordinated and slightly ramshackle type sanitarium, which had been added to, remodeled, face-lifted, publicly decried and also defended, condemned and reinstated — in short, an architect's nightmare to deal with. Yet my boss continued to work with this thing, patiently and conscientiously. Some time after yet another 1-room addition was completed (construction cost $8,000; architect's fee $480; architect's cost $1,600), his office obtained the commission to design a new 2.6 million dollar sanitarium to replace this monstrosity. As I said, it was the impressive after-effect which gave me much to ponder.

Shortly after I opened my own doors one of the first commissions I managed to receive was the design of a representative entrance to a university campus. The project was quite small but I recalled the sanitarium episode and put my entire heart into it. Even though it did not materialize, the administration was obviously pleased with my performance. Soon thereafter, a slightly larger commission followed: the remodeling of an old building into a small theater. This work was completed within the budget and wholly successful. The next one from the same client was exactly 100 times larger and within the span of a few years, the building volume for this client had reached many millions per year.

In the second case, the architect who is already established and is being asked to

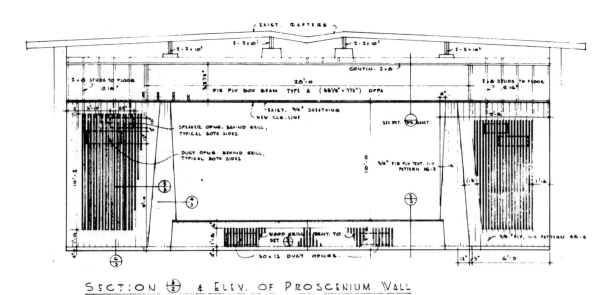

SECTION ②/2 BTWN. BOX BM & STEEL BM
1/4 = 1-0

SECTION ⑤/2 & ELEV. OF PROSCENIUM WALL
1/4 = 1-0

Fig. 2.1 A drawing typical of "omnium-gatherum," showing existing new work and demolition. The importance is its simplified solution and clear, uncluttered, readable drawings which will result in economical construction bids. The lower half shows also a partial elevation of a stage.

Fig. 2.2 The completed "omnium-gatherum." No patron of this intimate theater considered it a remodeling, but a wholly conceived functional and pleasant environment.

carry through omnium-gatherum projects would labor under an illusion if he believed that such work is below his dignity and only suitable for the beginning or so-called small architect. Owners know only too well what large commissions mean to an architect and are quite capable of guessing that often substantial profits are being made. They also know that omnium-gatherum are potential loss projects to the architect. It is therefore a matter of noblesse oblige that the architect should be willing to perform the less pleasant tasks as well.

An executive of a public institution with an annual building volume of many millions once told me of one of their principal architects. The firm was consistently honored with a large share of the projects. At the beginning this architect was willing to provide a balanced service, for example, he did his share of omnium-gatherum. Increasingly however, the executive told me, the institution encountered resistance whenever the architect was asked to take on certain smaller projects. The final straw was added when one of the chiefs of the architectural firm casually remarked to an engineer of the institution that his firm was too large to "fool with that kind of stuff." Word quickly reached the executive and, for some unexplainable reason, the institution for several years had no suitable project for this architectural firm.

Concluding, a vast portion of commissions are obtained through a small beginning with a large client. Once the architect has the confidence of the owner and is employed steadily, small projects must be taken along with the larger ones.

Regardless of the kind of owner, the architect is always expected to perform such omnium-gatherum work with his fullest interest, devotion and enthusiasm. It is the attitude the client looks for in his architect.

Ulterior Obligation

In the grand framework of the architect's significance, he has indeed an ulterior reason to concern himself with the smaller and more complex projects. For the shaping of the visible environment the architect claims leadership. Logically, therefore, he must concern himself with the entire range of structures and cannot choose according to convenience.

If he refuses to take omnium-gatherum under his wings, someone else will have to take care of it. Since the someone else must be a contractor, moonlighting draftsman or layman, the results are likely to be less contributory to a cultural environment, thus depressing the whole field of architecture. Any street in this country bears witness to this statement. It would be deceiving to point the finger at anyone outside the profession. True, architects have lost a good deal of control over the shaping of Main Street, U.S.A., but the loss is partly self-inflicted.

I have often had a prospective client in my office who wanted services for a small project which would probably not amount to more than a few hundred dollars. Invariably the client would conclude his story by saying, almost apologetically, "... but I suppose you don't ever do small projects like this one." I have made it a policy of my office to accept any size project and treat all with equal interest and thoroughness. It has proved to be very beneficial, particularly on account of the many referrals that have emanated from the practice. Omnium-gatherum rarely becomes a financial loss. Most of all, however, it has helped broaden the good image of my office. One must never lose sight that the well-faring office rests upon a wide base of many and well inclined clients.

Extracurricular Activities

The effective architect should engage in activities related to his profession, such as serving on citizens' planning committees and building and advisory boards, partaking in discussions and study sessions, and giving talks. It serves the twofold purpose of keeping one abreast of the current thoughts and needs of society and it also enhances the good image of architecture. Last but not least, it publicizes one's name with positive connotation.

As is well known, the cost of promotion which must be absorbed by those projects which materialize, is surprisingly high. One of the most significant contributors to the overhead of one's office is the principal's time spent on promotion.

The efficiency with which this time is being used is therefore quite important. Any participation on committees for example, or such things as the deliverance of speeches, should advisedly be concentrated upon those segments of society from which one makes one's livelihood.

It must always be remembered, however, that lending one's professional abilities to a non-profit cause is indirectly of great value to the profession. Strangely enough, when the motives are the purest, the indirect benefits become greatest.

One day a professor for graduate students in education called upon me with the request that I lecture about school auditoriums. Although I had little time to spare, I did oblige and, with disgracefully few preparations, delivered a lecture to a group of school principals and teachers in preparation for their doctoral degree.

Several years later I received an invitation from a school district I did not even know existed, to meet with the school board for the purpose of discussing the construction of an auditorium. Two weeks later I had a contract with them. It happened that the superintendent of the district was among the graduate students to whom I had lectured several years before.

chapter 3

The Client:
How to Keep Him

$\mathbf{D}$URING THE CREATION of a building, no one must work closer together than the architect and his client. Much of the success depends on the harmonious relationship between the two. It is therefore important that the architect know his clients, understand their feelings, peculiarities, anxieties, and anticipate their behavior.

Clients fall into three broad categories: private, semi-public and public. The special case of great significance in our society is the building committee. The chapter discusses all of these clients and those facets which are of interest to the architect. In conclusion, three basic guidelines of how to obtain an adequate fee are outlined.

The Private Owner

The most important concern to the private client is the direct personal responsibility he is assuming for the funds to be expended on a project. If the project is the kind which is to produce revenues, his responsibility is directed towards the simple goal of making a profit from the investment. For projects with no direct monetary return, such as religious, health, or welfare buildings, or private educational institutions, his responsibility is directed more towards the wise and judicious application of the funds.

Because of this responsibility, the owner's key behavior is caution. Reaching every facet of the building project, his caution is greatest in the initial decisions of What, How Large, Where and When. As the project assumes more tangible forms, his caution penetrates into details of financial feasibility, building technology and internal appointments. The caution does not recede until the building nears completion.

His second most important concern is that of efficiency of the investment. The efficiency is so important that most projects must completely submit to it.

For buildings with no direct return, his concern is primarily to attain maximum desirability and usefulness, that is, how efficiently the prime function is represented in the building.

These motives of behavior of the private owner must clearly be understood and also accepted by the architect. Many architects can't grasp the sober demand for a profitable building or simply usefulness. These architects tend to battle for the building rather than the interests of the owner. While this is often necessary and in the long-range view of interest to the owner, it can lead to rapid alienation at the very beginning. One of the first requirements to keep the owner is to understand his seemingly senseless and tasteless demands for a money maker rather than a Greek temple.

The client has, in this respect, a viewpoint almost completely opposite to that of the architect. He has no interest in aesthetics for its own sake in a building which is to produce a profit. He is likely to demand something which, to his untrained mind, represents aesthetics, something describable as "jazz," or "razzmatazz." He demands a dose of it in his building, but only sufficient to be competitive. Other clients set their idea of aesthetics on a higher level, that of good materials and a show of wealth — marble, stainless steel and perhaps luminous ceilings. Eventually, of course, there are the few private clients who seek the truer concept of aesthetics in real architecture and tasteful appointments.

It is most important that the architect realize that the average client is untrained in matters of aesthetics and, rather than surrendering to his innocent but often preposterously misconceived ideas, the architect should persuade him to accept the premises of lasting and real architecture instead of dazzling fashion. At the moment when the client is looking for a design of beauty, he is most receptive to the arguments outlined in chapter 5.

The Semi-Private Client

Under this category fall clients for those buildings which are subject to group financing, group decisions and group operation. For buildings of this kind the client is usually a multi-membered board, representing a much greater number of people. The common vector of these boards is, in the final analysis, quite similar to that of an individual with respect to the building and its purpose. The building board or committee is therefore referred to in the subsequent discussion simply as the client.

For these types of buildings, with the exception of the utilitarian kind, the client seeks a show of wealth first, utility next and aesthetics last. Luxury equals aesthetics to him. Quality is of less importance since he cannot enjoy it. This must be understood by the architect. An excessive insistence upon material quality will only irritate the client.

To private clients administering utilitarian buildings such as Y.M.C.A.'s, hospitals, even schools the other two attributes are important: first, maximum usefulness, then sturdiness, and luxury last. The funds are to be spent for a specific purpose — nothing else. Matters of aesthetics have no place if they take funds away from the intrinsic purpose. To keep this client, the architect must, with the best of his ability, seek the most efficient use of funds. The challenge to create tastefully under these circumstances is even greater and a good solution much appreciated by most clients.

The Committee

One of the most common clients of any practicing architect is the building committee. As shallow and bizarre as are the results it obtains, as inefficient and regressive as are its conceptions, the building committee is part of our democratic society. It is the rule of the people in miniature decisions.

What is the substance of a board, a committee? Why is it considered necessary? What does it accomplish within its own limitations?

The committee's prime purpose is a representation of as many interests as possible. In its collective judgment it is to create a democratically acceptable compromise of all interests. Furthermore, it is the commonly accepted belief that the plurality of wisdom will be the best safeguard against errors in the planning. Committees almost always speak for large groups of people, but in a few isolated cases for one supremely powerful person who appointed the committee. In nearly all instances the committee also has the watchdog function and is, in a diffused way, responsible to the larger group for the outcome of its activities. Quite generally, however, the committee's decisions made during the stage of planning are, good or bad, completely forgotten the moment the committee dissolves, or, in the case of a standing committee, upon final approval of the drawings.

As I said, the committees are there to represent interests, to safeguard, and to make decisions. These decisions may be of two kinds: advisory, stating wishes rather than demands; and dictatorial, simply ordering that their demands be carried out. If the committee is reasonable (and ethical) it will not make any dictatorial demands unless it first alters the terms of reference, such as the budget or the program, to accommodate the change of concept. If the committee, on the other hand, is emboldened by collective security, it tends to extend its powers and will impose any demands its members make, without a change of terms. The architect is, fortunately, not quite helpless. Even a hardened committee with only remnants of moral responsibility fears one thing — to be threatened with true responsibility for their decisions.

I had, in the course of several years, dealt repeatedly with a standing committee of a diocese. The committee was composed of old-to-ancient clergymen, entirely accustomed to sit in judgment over the architect rather than advising and guiding. Few architects were known to survive more than two projects, because they resigned in discouragement never again to come in contact with this committee. The committee was wholly unaccustomed to resistance to any dictate. Its decisions and demands on my earlier projects were irritating but fortunately not important. Finally, on a church which I designed, their demands became outrageous, and here I made my capital error: I opposed them openly. The ensuing friction reached the point where I had to compromise lest I be forced to give up the project. In the decisive meeting, after one of the members had introduced a lengthy motion containing a string of the most infuriating and imbecilic dictates I had ever heard, I demurely asked for the floor and made the following simple statement. I said, "Gentlemen (I wanted to say 'rascals in black'), before you vote on this motion I must inform you that you will have assumed with its passage, responsibility for the safety, budget and aesthetics of the building." Thereupon followed an unusually long discussion with the outcome that the motion was quietly withdrawn. Two things saved the situation: the direct imposition of naked responsibility and an intentionally dramatized form of delivery.

A distinctive feature of the building committee is that it will rarely oppose any of its member's requests unless controversy is induced artificially. The reason for this is that the committee has a common "foe" and instinctively will put up a united front.

The members must agree among themselves and will, to guarantee unity, let each have his pet request. It is precisely this feature which reminds me of the definition of a camel as a horse put together by a committee.

The Committee and the Architect

What can the architect do to prevent the camelization of his horse without losing rapport, and eventually the client?

First, the architect must have the answers. A committee member who raises a question has, if the architect is unable to provide a satisfactory answer, scored a point for the committee. If this happens more than once, sufficient doubt has been cast upon the architect's design (and possibly his ability) to make his position difficult, if not untenable. It is unfortunate that most committees seem to have at least one member who has a grudge against architects. This member will go out of his way to set traps for the architect. It is therefore necessary to isolate him early and be well prepared to answer him.

Apart from having the answers, there is a second and more dramatic means of defense at the architect's disposition. It is a form of counter-offensive in which he must begin to sow doubts in the minds of the others about the good judgment of the querulous member. This is done by taking that member's questions or demands very seriously and discussing them at great length until they are thoroughly discredited. Before doing so, one must, of course, be certain that the motive of the question was indeed harassment.

Also, with the exception of the rare dramatic or strategic moment, the architect's language must be kept to the layman's level. To conduct the discussion in a "snow job" manner is transparent to everybody and usually backfires sadly. If words like "concept," "precept," "rhythm," "proportion," "theme," etc. must be used, a short explanation of their meaning should be given. If this is done tactfully and elegantly, a committee can be persuaded and the majority will begin to ignore the contrary questioner.

If the architect's relationship with the building committee has become tenuous, it may be necessary to induce division within the group. Before doing so, however, the architect must be sure that his standpoint is wholly correct, fair and defensible. The mechanics of inducing division follows an elementary strategy. Here is an example: A seven-member board outnumbers the architect seven to one. To overcome their opposition, he must win first one and then another to his point of view. To do so, he must meet the members individually. When stripped of the collective security of assemblage, most committee members are not only vulnerable but meek. Once a trend away from opposition begins, the architect's views are almost sure to prevail.

In recapitulation, the following main guidelines should be followed in dealing with building committees:

a) At whatever stage of progress, the presentation of the architect's case must be well prepared and rehearsed.

b) Answers must be exhaustive. If questions concern a stage of progress not yet reached, as they so often do, the committee must be told so and given a clear idea what kind of questions can be answered now and what kind later on. It can be disastrous if answers are given in matters which are not wholly thought through.

c) If a cantankerous member emerges, his arguments must be countered as soon as possible, otherwise the situation can rapidly get out of hand.

d) If no other means are possible, the stratagem of division among the board members can be put into effect.

In the discussion of boards, I have primarily concerned myself with the negative aspects of the subject. I must, in fairness to our society, also mention that there are boards staffed by highly competent members who, with great efficiency, can make substantial improvements in almost any proposal put before them.

The Public Owner

There are several classes of the public owner as client. Their common denominator is the administration of public funds. The responsibility is different from that of the private owner since funds no longer have to be repaid nor do they need to show a direct profit. The responsibility for spending rests with the wisdom, efficiency and intelligence with which the investments are made. This client's natural check is the press, primarily the daily newspaper. Because of the client's sensitivity to public opinion, much of his thinking and reacting is directed towards public approval of his decisions.

This client exists in all gradations from the school board, with its almost personal responsibility to the voters of the district, to the federal governmental agency with a general sensitivity to public opinion at a national, almost statistical level.

This client's goals and objectives are largely determined by his proximity to the public. For example, the school board is subject to personal criticism and will therefore, in natural reflex, first of all seek the most quantity for the dollar.

As this client's contact with the public becomes more distant, his aims shift more towards quality. School boards, for example, give only lip service to the questions of quality and maintenance cost; a state agency, on the other hand, is quite concerned with maintenance cost and gives consideration to adequate spaces and acceptable appearance.

The federal agencies have arrived at the state where certain high standards of materials, sufficient spaces for functions, conservative aesthetics (to please all people) and good masterplanning are standard repertory. On this level the client is primarily concerned with the outcome and less with cost because he is rarely criticized for over-spending on an isolated issue but quickly accused of having made unworkable decisions.

The Architect and the Public as Client

The school board knows that the only yardstick of the public is the square foot cost. If, in 15 years, maintenance costs equal the original construction cost, the public will be uninterested. Aesthetics are generally considered wastefulness. While the attitudes toward these three attributes — original cost, maintenance and aesthetics — are stated here in greatly simplified form, they nevertheless show the architect that on this level his client is indeed the community, its mood, its affluency and behavior.

About midpoint between the community as a client and the federal agency are the state, county and city governments. Nothing arouses the interest of the press more than capital outlay and bond program projects. Criticism is leveled at just about everything: cost, quality and aesthetics. Also, nowhere is politics thicker than in the local jungle of "connections" and "friends of mine." The milieu is quite exciting for the architect. Everybody can be found on these levels of public administration; the crusader and the obsequious sycophant; the cultured lay-architect and the barbarous politician; the classically honorable civil servant and the cunning finagler, all with whom the architect is expected to work. He must therefore acquaint himself with his immediate surroundings and, as far as possible, the influences beyond. I have found it absolutely invaluable to isolate myself, at least philosophically, and to assume a posture of individualism — the abstract professional, the colorful architect, who can be appreciated by most and be reckoned with where necessary. Because this level still permits, even requires, the individualist, it is most important also that the architect retain the image as the professed masterplanner of mankind's physical environment.

As the final stage of elevation, the federal governmental agency has two characteristics of great significance to the architect. One is a generally receptive attitude towards better architecture; purpose before cost, together with long-range view and planning. The second is the regrettable submissiveness to highest political pressures. As additional but marginal observations: this client works and operates according to preplanned schema, charted out manuals, red tape and paper work. Furthermore, time is almost never of the essence. If this client has been annoyed, entire departmental structures will turn to ice, unforgiving forever. The mistake of degrading or ridiculing civil servants is simply not made by the effective architect. It is essential that he understand the direction of thinking, the necessity of rules and the emotional characteristics of civil servantism. If he does, his lot will be an acceptable one, for few segments of society have so great an interest in or understanding of the architect's thinking.

Understanding the Client

Sometimes clients appear more like paying enemies than business partners. Their caution, even suspicion, seems strange and quite unfounded. The sudden shift from rapport to repudiation, the seemingly uncalled for criticism of one's work, often echo actions by an architect who has no real understanding of his client.

Clients are not invariably right nor architects always wrong, but the architect must understand the source of the client's irritation — his near total commitment to the architect and his professional performance. Once confidence has been infracted, relations often deteriorate rapidly. The client feels cornered and eventually enraged.

The architect can best understand a client's feeling if he places himself in his position. Any architect who has had to select another architect for a project, where its success remained his responsibility, has experienced some of the anxiety: did I select the best man? what will his first design concepts be like? will his drawings and specs be in order, has he chosen the most elegant or economical structure? will he be within the budget? were his consultants worth anything? is he going to supervise properly? how many additive change orders are going to be necessary? what can I do if I don't like his design? To be sure, careful selection of the architect is the best way to allay these fears, but the client is a layman and not necessarily aware of the whole picture.

The effective architect should therefore endeavor strongly to understand his client's feeling by continuously attempting to see the situation through his eyes. Even if the client's concerns are unjustified and his conclusions wrong and harmful to himself, he can be reasoned with if he's convinced the architect is for him, and is in fact his friend.

For the private and semi-public client, this applies primarily to the project. For the governmental client, the understanding must be a more personal one. The architect should never forget that the representative, who is but one member in a vast system, is indeed an individual, with personal interest in what he is doing and accomplishing. Impatience or conceit in the architect, even if directed more at the system than at the individual, is usually considered a personal affront by the civil servant.

The Course of Client/Architect Relationship

The course of the relationship should be, and is in most instances, a happy one providing the architect performs well and the client pays the fee correctly.

The relationship begins at the interview, a strenuous beginning for both. The client makes his most important decision for his project and is quite naturally troubled. The architect, on the other hand, goes through mental anxiety over whether or not he has presented his case successfully enough to be awarded the project. Once the decision is made the sun breaks through for both. I, as an architect, consistently highlight this moment with a bottle of Scotch to each of my associates.

Then begins the well-known period of the honeymoon. Concepts and thoughts solidify, programs are set down, the initial meetings take place. At this point the first, but very slight, turbidness might appear. It usually happens because both begin to show their true color. The client usually presents his ideas, which the architect considers an intrusion into his métier. He, on the other hand, is prompted to propose preconceived ideas and sometimes begins to show a certain impatience and rigidity of thinking. At this point the architect must accept the position of the listener. I have found it best to make a great many notes of what the client says or wants and openly play the role of professional who strives to acquaint himself with the total picture as the client sees it. In these early stages, the architect should never become specific, or he runs the risk of the client's mind solidifying around trivialities. Later these may become interfering substances in the total design.

About midway between first meetings and the graphic presentation of the concept, it is often the architect's turn to become a bit sour. Oddly enough the reason is the absence of a written agreement, a situation which is self-inflicted because he did not have the courage to submit a contract but hopefully waited for the right moment. There is a little strategy for the timid professional which I, who sometimes also went too long without an agreement, have accepted as quite successful. Immediately after being commissioned, I write my client a note of appreciation which contains among pleasing words all the necessary dates to define the verbal agreement. Subsequently, I maintain an active written record and frequent correspondence. It does not take very long and the records would be enough to "sue on."

If everything has gone well so far the unveiling of the first design is the highlight of the honeymoon. Two points should be observed to preclude any possible disturbance at this stage of the game. First, it is wise to give the client an early hint what the design will be like. If this reaction tester obtains favorable response, it not only virtually assures acceptance of the design but heightens the client's appetite in just the right way. Secondly, the unveiling of the design must be well prepared and executed. The presentation must have all necessary elements: first the recapitulation of the project's determinants, followed by a theoretical (but short) treatise on the approach and its solution. Then it is best to reveal the design from within, starting at a given point in the plan. This can be expanded to the site or master plan. As the culminating event, the unveiling of the exterior appearance should be kept to the last.

From here the first real difficulty may arise when the client subsequently begins to turn architect himself and introduces a string of changes which, right or wrong, are never to the liking of the architect. This possibility can be minimized through close communication at the earlier planning stages. Should the situation, however, come about, the architect must do everything to terminate it as soon as possible. Otherwise, the project will begin to disintegrate. The architect should therefore take several steps with both patience and firmness:

a) Incorporate the client's wishes as well as possible. The architect must act here primarily as professional advisor.
b) Constantly remind the client that certain changes will increase the budget.
c) Divide the project into segments. Within the segments changes can be made but the project's external limits and relationships should remain untouched.
d) The client's written approval should be obtained as soon as possible. In most cases this will force him to refrain from random groping.

For the continued success of the good client/architect relationship it is absolutely essential that the project be completely defined in the design and so approved by the client. The architect is wise to inform his client repeatedly that once the contract documents are on the way, changes are very costly.

The next milestone is taking bids and its aftermath. This is discussed thoroughly in Chapter 8.

The second to last subject demanding attention in the architect/client relationship is supervision. There is no client who is of the opinion that the architect is over-extending his services in this phase. On the contrary, a lack of supervision is generally claimed. The effective architect does well to explain to his client at the start of construction the entire procedure of supervision, in particular that the man he sees on the job site is only part of the work force employed on this project. Secondly, the client should be kept well informed through bi-weekly or monthly reports. What the client fears is being deserted and left to argue with the contractor. On the other hand, clients are often lured into dealing directly with contractors. Since this can be most detrimental to the project, the architect, for once, must show excitement and make it clear to the client that he is now assuming responsibilities himself. That usually brings such dealings to an abrupt end.

The final issue concerns the warranty period. If the client has had tendencies to feel deserted during construction, the feeling is likely to change to abandonment in the year following completion. As will be noted in the following chapter, continued good relations with the client are, during this time, of greatest importance.

Concluding, I feel compelled to mention that there are clients not worth dealing with. Fortunately, they are rare. But when they emerge they can make the architect's life miserable. Projects like this are invariably carried in red ink, even before the stage of design is completed. So far I have had two clients of this kind — unethical, antagonistic, unreasonable, and insolent. I completed both projects, with substantial losses, many a sleepless night and a stomach turned to knots. In retrospect, it would have been better to part company in the early stages, to devote time and energy to more useful enterprises.

Fees

In the relationship of client and architect it is essential to the former to assure himself of the adequacy of the latter's services, and it is the latter's justified concern to receive a fair fee.

I have touched upon the subject in other chapters and will augment it here with some general observations.

Clients are, by and large, rather uninformed about fees and their justifications. What they see and comprehend is what they concede merits remuneration. Beyond that, the client must be educated. Therefore, when the fee is discussed at the beginning, all aspects should be brought to his attention. Specifically, the following facts should be explained:

a) The work force necessary to design and supervise a project; that this force consists of many others besides the architect and his staff; that there are structural, mechanical, electrical and plumbing engineers, and their staffs who are involved. Sometimes they are augmented by specialists and other consultants. The architect's fee, as should be explained, must be divided into several parts.

b) Some picture of the time and hours which must go into a project can be presented. The architect should, however, in advance, have his figures in order to substantiate costs per hour, overhead, special expense. In its simplest form, one can, for example, divide a fee of $60,000.00 by the average hourly rate of all staff plus a given percentage of overhead to obtain a plausible number of hours. If it appears appropriate, the engineering fees could first be deducted as lump sums.

c) The relationship to the overall project cost should be explained. Most clients do not understand that bids alone can vary between 6% and 10%, usually more than the entire architect's fee. Also, the contractor's profit is often equal or larger than that fee. This does not mean that either is wrong, but simply reveals the real relationship. For example, two methods express the same end result but give quite a different picture:

1)			2)		
Construction Cost	$ 950,000.		Construction cost	1,100,000.
Built-in furniture	35,000.		Architect's fee, 6%	66,000.
Contractor's overhead	60,000.		Project cost	1,166,000.
Contractor's profit	55,000.			
Architect's fee	44,000.			
Engineer's fee	22,000.			
Project cost	1,166,000.			

To obtain a higher fee commensurate with a more complex project is often possible. Most architects, however, fear that if they ask for a higher fee the client will drop them altogether. I have found this not to be true if put to the test.

One particular project in the earlier years of my practice is a typical case. It was a small hospital, partly new construction, partly internal remodeling; a difficult and messy thing. The fee in the state was limited to 6% by law, but by special arrangement could be extended upwards. As could be expected, the figure of 6% for all public buildings had long since become the sacred meeting ground between owner and architect. The hospital board was no exception and had obviously no intention of changing its viewpoint. Yet, I knew the project could not be carried out for 6%; either my work would be substandard or I would lose money.

In the final interview, I requested the standard fee, but exempted the mechanical and electrical engineering for the portion to be remodeled, i. e., the cost of engineering could be in addition to the 6%. I supported my request with a fairly detailed explanation of the complexity of mechanical and electrical remodeling and the cost of recording the existing construction. Furthermore, I explained that, according to the owner-architect agreement, the owner must furnish plans of the existing structure, plans which could be very costly, and that the responsibility for the correctness of these plans was theirs. Thus I had confronted the board with facts they could not ignore regardless who the architect would be. Furthermore, I knew that the proposal was fair to all concerned, something the board soon recognized.

As a result I obtained the commission with an increased fee. The approach of fairness paired with strategy has since become most valuable as a business tool, in particular in the negotiation of adequate fees.

chapter 4

How to Obtain
Commissions

For ALL EXISTING and future buildings, there are owners. This chapter discusses the systematic approach to a project; first is the publicizing of one's firm; then the isolation of a specific project, followed by the necessary steps to obtain a commission for it. The chapter deals also with all essential facets of the first personal contact, the follow-up, the interview, and periodic visits to potential clients.

Frequently architects lose clients. Methods are discussed of how to regain their confidence and how to continue after a difficult beginning.

Competitions are often overlooked as a source of commissions. Presented is a brief treatise on why some architects shun competitions, how to arouse professional support for and how to pursue plans to hold competitions.

The chapter concludes with a catalog of major building owners, bodies or persons who will select architects, contacts for first information, and types of buildings involved.

The Search for the Target

The first step in the quest for a commission is to find an unbuilt building, a project under consideration. There are three basic methods by which the building project can be discovered.

General Broadcasting

The first is the general broadcasting of one's existence and abilities, with the anticipation that one or more recipients of the announcement are in need of an architect. The broadcasting can best be done by a systematic mailing campaign of tastefully designed cards, stating firm name, field of activities, possible specialization. Furthermore, a motivating reason for the mailing may be used; such as special accomplishments – like an outstanding building, a new field of specialization, a new associate, or change of address. Or, mailing may consist of suitable brochures.

In any campaign specific targets must be chosen lest the action become ineffective. For example: if a firm specializes or plans to specialize in hospital work, the targets of the campaign should be hospital boards and administrators, and the material specifically tailored to arouse their interest. Likewise, if emphasis lies in the field of manufacturing plants, the mailing material should be designed to interest plant managers, corporate boards, owners, and property managers of industrial concerns.

The well-aimed broadcasting does two things; it places a firm's name on a list of potential architects and it also serves as a prelude to a personal visit. I have in my practice conducted mailing campaigns with considerable success. All were based on the propagation of a new design, system or concept and all prepared in a brief, informative three- to five-page leaflet. The mailing recipients were always carefully selected to find as many potential clients as possible. Furthermore, I have found it psychologically better if the mailing had a pronounced overtone that no answer was expected. While there is always the possibility that someone is in need of just this kind of help precisely at the moment of mailing, the mailing campaign should not be considered a failure if no immediate commission is obtained.

Because mailing campaigns are a definite contact, like all contacts they must be repeated. Therefore, if an architect decides to start this form of broadcasting, he must continue. A large architectural and engineering firm in Europe, which specializes in certain industrial plants, developed a highly systematic procedure. For each completed project, the firm prepared a three-page brochure, showing plans, basic technical and cost data, and two to three photographs. A good number, perhaps 24 such projects, were placed in a tastefully designed ring binder. At the initial visit of a representative of this firm, this collection was presented to the executives of the industrial plants. Subsequently, at the rate of perhaps once in two months, this firm produced additional brochures from completed projects and mailed these to the recipients of the original collection. About every six months a personal visit to most prospective clients was undertaken. At these visits a specific point was made to discuss a previous project for which a leaflet had been mailed. Thus the firm ascertained whether the client indeed studied as well as kept their material. Invariably some questions had arisen which made these visits very pleasant and productive.

Eventually, a prospective client had become so familiar with the ability and performance of this firm that a commission was given. After fifteen years of existence this firm was working on over fifty multi-million dollar projects, in nearly all parts of the world.

Isolation of a Specific Project

The second method is the search for a definite and real project. To discover and isolate this project so that a plan of approach can be prepared, several ways and means are practical and useful.

It is generally correct that he who has earliest knowledge of a project has leading advantage. Therefore, the search for a project should be concentrated on those which are in the first stages of discussion. Since most projects require years to mature, it is therefore necessary to accept the basic premise: the project "x" years hence is as much of interest to me as work breaking next month. The search begins with the analysis of plans, growth pattern and trend of institutions, organizations, or groups engaged in building. In doing so, building projects of immediate and long-range planning soon become evident.

Let me cite two typical examples: banks and institutions of higher learning. Usually, banks have a main office, regional offices and branch banks. The system must adjust itself to population increases, population shifts and free-world banking habits. As a fluid structure, the main office will require a periodic expansion, possibly a new headquarters every few decades. Regional offices and branch banks are usually designed to saturation of a given residential area and only their numbers will, therefore, be increased. Also, every so often outdated facilities must be replaced. An architect entering this system should, in careful study, isolate the future buildings with respect to "soon," "several years from now," and the long-range view. Thus he obtains valuable knowledge of the number, size and kinds of buildings and their timing.

In a university, the ever-increasing enrollment and changing educational techniques demand constant building activities. Since buildings are usually funded well after (often several years) their need has been demonstrated to satisfaction, the isolation of a building must start at a time when the need has first become evident. Once the point of funding has been reached, the architect has usually already been chosen. While universities for obvious reasons are reluctant to reveal their entire plans to any architect, complete master plans which are accurate for at least the immediate future invariably exist. Nevertheless, with caution and tact, the architect can learn of specific projects and begin to concern himself with them.

The Swing Around the Country

One of the most useful methods of keeping abreast of project planning in the wider community, such as a county or state, is a periodic swing around the country. The people to be visited should be those who are knowledgeable of the development and proposed plans of an area, and those who are potential builders themselves.

One of the best places in any community to gain a good overall picture is the office of city engineers, city managers and directors of public works. Their knowledge extends into all proposed (even in the distant future) plans within a community. School district superintendents are a second-best source of information. The very nature of their activities gives them personal and statistical insight into a given area's activity. A third source is bank managers. While very well informed about the commercial activity of an area, they are sometimes a bit reluctant to divulge information of possibly confidential (but very useful!) nature. To lessen the formality of a visit, it usually suffices to get in touch with one's own branch bank and obtain a recommendation from someone in the system who knows the manager.

Last but not least, one should follow up on all credible local leads. Only thus can a new and as yet unpublicized project be discovered.

One very significant aspect of the swing around the country is to see the same people again and again. Thus their confidence in the visiting architect becomes quite solid and information leading to projects soon begins to be volunteered. How often should the swing around the country be made? Well, that depends upon several things, such as geographical area encompassed, number of people to be visited, and kinds of visits. Generally, one should undertake the round trip every six to nine months.

No Discouragement Justified

How often has the reader learned either through a newspaper or magazine, or some "inside" information, that someone is preparing to build! He then no doubt went immediately into high gear in pursuit of this project, only to find that his colleague next door has had the contract in his pocket for some time already.

For the consolation of the reader — in the majority of cases it was sheer statistical probability. He simply knew someone you did not know, because he had different connections. You, with your specific field of knowledge, appear just as well connected to him. He is not necessarily smarter or better than you. For the sake of efficiency, one thing is true nevertheless: when a project has been picked up by the press, it is usually too late to expect the commission.

The Informative Personal Visit

Prior to the prepared visit with the decision-making executive, a sort of personal reconnaissance is often an invaluable intermediate step. Purposefully, the contact should be with someone who can give the architect a picture of who is who, and what plans exist. However, the information obtained should generally be taken with some caution, since a subordinate is rarely fully informed. Nevertheless, sufficient data can be gathered to formulate the first direct approach.

Isolation of the Executive

It is absolutely essential that eventually the executive or board members who have the authority to select the architect be located. To find these people there is simply no other way but to make extensive inquiries, preferably of more than one group, until the decision-making body has been firmly established. I would like to emphasize this point, since often contacting the less important person is cause for much inefficiency. One must ask one's way up, through and around, cautiously, tactfully, and with great persistence. The method must be entirely adapted to the situation: a personal reconnaissance trip, and inquiry through secondary channels (those who deal with a potential client, such as engineers or sales agencies), or sometimes through a simple direct telephone call to the highest level. To break into a giant system requires giant effort. Finding the decision-making regional official of a federal department often begins with a visit to the department headquarters at Washington, D.C. A search of this kind is often exasperating and lengthy, but it has high probability of success, if patience is maintained.

My experience has shown that caution is at this point very necessary, primarily because an inadvertently ill-prepared meeting, in which the architect has nothing to offer, is but a waste of time and is generally resented. This applies as much to meetings with high-ranking civil servants as with anyone else. An architect is sadly mistaken if he believes that they must listen to him because they are public servants, or that their habitual politeness to the unannounced intruder is a promise or commitment.

Knowing the Client's Plans

The effective architect has up to this point taken all necessary steps, except one, preparatory to making the actual personal approach.

This last step is a study and familiarization with the client's plans and problems. Most often this aspect is entirely neglected because of some misinterpretation of the code of ethics (precluding any work prior to an agreement) or because it is simply considered unnecessary. Both reasons are erroneous.

In particular, with client's who have employed or are employing other architects, the newcomer is up against the competition of someone who is already familiar with the client's plans and problems, and need not be trained first. Furthermore, he has made his mistakes and begins to pay off for the owner. The newcomer must not only be introduced to everything, but is likely to commit costly errors, at least at the beginning. If therefore the architect is already familiar with the client's plans, and if he has something new to offer, the entrée is infinitely easier.

The First Personal Contact

Having gained some insight into the client's set-up, structure of authority, intentions and plans, and having studied as much as possible about them, the architect is ready to seek an appointment for the first personal contact.

The first meeting is to present the architect's image, knowledge and usefulness to the prospective client in a most favorable light, and to obtain reliable, firsthand information to be used henceforth.

The impression the architect makes during this first meeting is most often decisive. It is, therefore, of greatest importance that this first encounter be a complete success. To make it so, he must be well prepared.

First it is necessary immediately to capture the interest of the other party. To be able to do so, one must show, without sales talk or persuasive pressures, that one is in a position to offer something the other party is looking for, something which is in his immediate field of interest. Even though the prospective client has not solicited the architect's visit, he has nevertheless a general interest in speaking with him: the architect might bring something valuable into the picture which others have not. The architect has thus a natural entrée which he should not spoil through carelessness. The information collected previously about a pending project must have been transformed into an orderly, comprehensive background in the architect's mind, from which he can state his ideas about the project. It is of relatively little consequence if this architect has repeated some things others have also said. The prospective client realizes that the first meeting will not necessarily spawn the great, new idea. If he hears a repetition of previous ideas, he will recognize it more as an affirmation, which will rank the architect equal with others. The orderliness with which the case is stated becomes then more important.

If enough time is available, it is usually better to begin with introduction of the firm. The client is naturally interested in the capability of the prospect before him, his accomplishments and his apparent business know-how. These subjects should, therefore, be the essence of a self-introduction.

From here, and as soon as practical, a rapid transition can be made to *medias res*. The discussion of the client's project can be approached with words such as "my thoughts concerning your project are . . .," or "the uniqueness of your project challenges existing concepts and may well call for an approach such as . . ." There is no deception in the latter words; all projects are in themselves unique, something owners do like to hear. One point should be observed: many people like to talk more than listen. If the prospective client is of this type, listen to him by all means. You will flatter him and are likely to learn more.

The first meeting must be designed to leave with the prospective client the impression that he is dealing with an A-1 firm whose staff is:

    a) eminently qualified.
    b) very clear thinking.
    c) capable of producing original and innovative ideas.

If this image is left behind, along with well-chosen brochure material, the architect has made an excellent impression.

The Follow-Up

Shortly after the first personal contact, it is not only perfectly in order to see the prospective client again but is indeed quite necessary. An owner scarcely will hand out a project as the result of one visit, not even governmental agencies with sophisticated selection procedure will. An owner rarely feels irritated, providing, of course, the first meeting created a conducive climate for any subsequent get togethers. The follow-up need not be pretense. It is always best to make a clear and honest restatement of interest on the owner's project.

Nothing at the Moment

It is generally the rule that a prospective client says that he does not have a project on hand, for which to commission the architect who is passing by — be it because he really hasn't one, or because he has no desire to reveal his hand just yet. This client is likely to become more specific in subsequent meetings. The effective architect must recognize this and regard his introductory visit as just that. The owner with "nothing at the moment," should be revisited in well-chosen intervals and should be reapproached by letter and printed data, in short be subjected to a well laid-out campaign with the key note, "I would like to work for you. I am interested in your project." It is surprising how many owners will eventually commission this architect with a starter project.

After the first follow-up it is good strategy to introduce some variations into the otherwise banal purpose of the meeting. One of the most useful methods is an interest in the prospective client's person, such as hobbies, or professional or business accomplishments.

I recall visiting one of my best clients five times over a span of three years and writing him at least that many times. For each visit I had a variation in the approach, ranging anywhere from a discussion about the paper he had written to doing him a small favor and, of course, an invitation to the obligate businessman lunch.

The Interview

The interview is one of the most common procedures by which to select an architect, when a building project has assumed tangible form. He is then invited to appear before the owner for the sole purpose of being evaluated as a potential candidate for the project.

Of all the moments in the course of aspiring for the project, this is by far the most important. Preparation for the interview should be much like an actor's for opening night: weeks if not months are spent to prepare for a few score minutes of actual performance. It is one of the two moments of truth in the architect's life: the interview and the bid opening.

The architect to be interviewed must bear in mind a few basic points which are of decisive consequence. First he must be fully cognizant that he is competing — plain, primitive and unadulterated — with his colleagues. Because a selling job has to be done, the artist- or scientist-type architect is nearly completely out of his element, the business architect on the other hand is right in it. This, however, need not concern the first two types. The client is accustomed to the insinuative powers of business psychology, and at least partly immune. What interests him is the personality, as he imagines the architect to be.

Secondly, the architect must recognize that the client is in the buyer's market — analyzing and comparing — that he is a person with feelings, tastes, weaknesses, judging a good part on a nonlogical, instinctive level. The client can only compare on the basis of what he sees and hears in the short period of the interview. Of course, there are supporting facets, such as brochures, previous owners' recommendations; but the "in" or "out" is being decided on a personal level.

Thirdly, the client is looking for "his" architect. He hopes with each new candidate that this might be his man. Therefore, he is acutely interested in everything the architect says. He may be tired from having interviewed six other firms, but will almost always treat everybody with equal interest. It is of no consequence in which sequence the architects are being interviewed, since no one has the advantage. The first one may meet a fresher owner, but by the time he has reached number eight, the impressions of the previous candidates begin to fade. The architect remembered will be the one who said and presented something outstanding, exceptionally to the point and useful.

I have frequently observed that those who entered the interview self-assured, almost careless, rarely got the job. This form of behavior is insincere and will be sensed by the owner. A tongue-tied, even clumsy opening is not necessarily a disadvantage – the owner is not ignorant of the mental tension under which the architect is laboring. A wan smile is better than a political grin – relaxing humor, if used at all, should be left for the later part of the interview.

What should one say when, for example, a member of a committee introduces one and then simply throws the ball to the architect ". . . and now Mr. Archdrafter will make his presentation"?

What must come now had better be well rehearsed. First, one should give a brief but lively picture of one's firm, its length of existence, major projects (two to three usually suffice if they are fairly well known), specialization, and some idea of the size of one's office. Speaking of size, many owners use this as a yardstick of capacity or even ability. If one feels one may be eliminated because of insufficient staff, it is better either to make a virtue out of the smaller office by emphasizing the individual attention for each project or to quote the size of office in terms of building volume per year.

This introduction can be followed by a circumscription of one's firm's philosophy and approach to architecture and construction. From this beginning a direct transition may be made to the project under consideration. The architect may speak at length and in depth about the project, but what he says must be comprehensive and orderly, showing thorough knowledge of the material. The discussion should be concluded with a statement containing some original thoughts about the project.

Depending on circumstances and mood, the owners might like to see some pictures of the architect's work even before the discussion of the project commences. In this case the introduction can be concluded with a brief display of large photos (the larger the better). I have found a portfolio with 11″ x 14″ photographs most practical and also most impressive. Even if the same pictures can be found in the firm's brochure, an impressive portfolio with attractive pictures is always effective. I have taken, for certain interviews, fully framed color prints right off the wall of my office and achieved spectacular success with them. Equally good are small but exquisite models. The architect must never forget that the owner prefers to see and hear interesting things, if only because it requires less effort. The more interesting and lively the presentation, the greater the attention.

A brochure should be given at the end – just one, for a well gauged effect. More can be supplied later. Your conclusion should be rapid and your departure without prolonged civilities. I have seen architects forever repeating themselves about their interest, their "happiness" to submit further information, and quite thoroughly making asses of themselves.

The words *brief, orderly, concise* are repeatedly used in the above. The elixir of a successful interview is indeed brevity and condensation of the subject matter into its essence.

Tenacity and Its Value

It cannot be stressed enough that consistent, untiring pursuance of a client and/or a project is in most cases the key to success. *Veni, vidi, vici* applies only to the largest firms, who by the sheer weight of their brochure can crush any local aspirant. However, tenacity paired with tact (a sort of agreeable peskiness) will eventually lead to the client's surrender.

One of my clients once told me that he gave a smaller building to an architect simply to get the man off his back, but was so pleased with the performance that he unhesitatingly gave him further and much larger buildings.

The Second Project

If everything went well on the first project, chances are even that when the next one comes along the architect will be recommissioned. But, in many cases, the first job does not go so flawlessly that the next project may be taken for granted, nor can one ever ignore competitive efforts of other architects. If then, some unpleasantries emerged during a project and other architects are attempting to break into the system, the matter of retaining the client's confidence becomes the primary challenge. The following example shows one possible approach to a successful solution.

Some years ago I designed a high school for an outlying district. At the end there were problems left to the client: a leaky roof, planters that did not drain properly, some differential settlement which caused entrance doors to bind and sundry other annoyances. Since the project was 150 miles from the next largest city, almost no corrective work was done.

I was fairly helpless. The deficiencies were only to the smallest degree my fault. Therefore, I decided to do everything possible to have things corrected and, through repeated visits, prove to the client that he was not left to himself. The result was interesting. While only one minor flaw was corrected, the client simply learned to live with the remaining ones. He also retained full confidence in my sincerity. When the time came to add to the school plant, the project was virtually handed to me on a silver platter. The significance of good communications cannot be overstressed. Without it the client would have chosen someone else to design the next building.

How to Regain the Client's Confidence

Unlike the instance related above, it happens not infrequently that at the completion of a project the architect and owner have fairly well separated. Perhaps the project ran over the budget, or supervision was a source of friction, or the outcome of the building was unexpected to the owner, but the simple fact remains that the client is now displeased with his architect. If another project is contemplated, chances are a different man will do the next building.

What means has the architect at his disposition to regain the client's confidence?

There are two simple points which the architect must learn if he wishes eventually to be taken back into the fold. First, he should never burn bridges no matter how great his longing for that heartwarming little fire. The client's expression of annoyance should not meet with amplified counter-offensive. It is best to let the client blow off steam and to make an effort to correct what can be corrected. The second issue is time itself. Given enough time, the unpleasantness is forgotten. Once the client has learned to live with the building, he has also grown to like it. Furthermore, the replacement architect may leave a worse taste, whereupon the memory of the first gradually grows fonder. Finally, the architect must stay in touch with client and project. This makes the greatest impression.

Competitions

I am not speaking here of the large kind, controlled by The American Institute of Architects, which is shunned by most owners because of unwieldiness and is regarded with jaundiced eyes by most architects.

I am speaking of the invited competition. While relatively rare, it is the fairest, most elegant and most professional means to receive a commission. For the client it has all the advantages he could wish for.

For the invited competition the owner selects a few architects (anywhere from three to perhaps twelve) who, on the strength of their credentials, are all technically qualified to perform the services contemplated. Each one of these contestants is then invited to enter a one- or two-stage competition. In the single stage one, the entry is presented in its final form. This method is very satisfactory if the program is written well and the number of contestants low (between three and five). The two-stage system may be used if a greater number participate. Their number is then reduced in the first stage, usually a conceptual form of entry. A few finalists will then compete for the project. Prizes, if given at all, are nominal, providing the winner will be commissioned.

The point for caution may be the make-up of the jury. The owner has the right to appoint whatever judges he may wish. They must be knowledgeable, have taste, be without excessive prejudices and not know whose entry is whose. In fact, absolute discretion is essential; otherwise the matter turns into an owner's shopping enterprise. Therefore, the architect, who is invited and expected to gamble considerable time, has a right to be assured of a flawless judging procedure. I should hasten to add that it is usually better for the competing architects if there is a decided minority of architects, if any, on the jury.

The system eliminates the often unpleasant business-type competition of stratagems and the interplay of politics, and places professional abilities in the foreground. The system is, for this reason alone, one which should as often as practical be proposed to building clients.

Catalog of Building Owners

In the following tables, the major sources from which commissions emanate are listed. The tables must, however, be regarded only as a general guide since procedures and habits vary with the locality. It is suggested that the reader prepare for himself similar listings for his own area.

CATALOG OF MAJOR BUILDING GROUPS

PUBLIC OWNER OF	BODY THAT SELECTS ARCHITECTS	BUILDINGS
Schools (High & Elementary)	Board of Education; (architect must be accepted by the administration). Contact: Superintendent, Business Manager	Classrooms, Laboratories, Gymnasium, Auditoriums, Libraries, Administrative Offices, Shops
Colleges	Administration; (selection of architect is approved by Board of Trustees). Contact: Vice President, Director of Physical Plant	Classrooms, Laboratories, Libraries, Gymnasiums, Fine Arts Centers, Student Centers, Offices
Universities	Administration; (selection of architect is approved by Board of Trustees). Contact: Vice President for Business, Director of Physical Plant	Libraries, Laboratories, Classrooms, Lecture Halls, Fine Arts and Student Centers, Housing, Auditoriums, Hospitals, Museums
Cities	City Council; Mayor; City Manager. Contact: City Manager, Director of Public Works (political connections helpful)	Administrative, Civic (Libraries, Museums, Parks, Arenas, Auditoriums), Police and Fire Stations, Airports, Utility Structures
County Government	Board of Supervisors, Department Heads. Contact: Clerk of the Board (Political connections important)	Courthouses, Hospitals, Recreations & Parks, Administrative Offices, Police Bldgs.
State Governments	Department Heads. Contact: Planning commission and individual dept. heads. (Award of larger commissions almost always through political connections)	Administrative Offices, Technical Utility Buildings, Jails & Reformatories, Courthouses, Parks
Federal Government	Departments; Architect is chosen by a group of officials connected with construction. Biggest builders: Armed Forces, General Services Administration, Post Office, Indian Affairs. Contact: Departmental Administration	Administrative Offices, Post Offices, Research and Indian Facilities, Parks, Housing, Hospitals, Shops (Military Base Facilities, which include all types of buildings needed by a society)

PRIVATE OWNER (GROUP OWNERSHIP)	BODY THAT SELECTS ARCHITECTS	BUILDINGS
Hospitals	Governing Board; Church Organizations, Doctors' Groups. Contact: Administrator	Hospitals, Clinics, Infirmaries, Sanatoriums, Nursing and Convalescent Homes
Church	Depending on denomination; Pastor, Building Committee, Bishop. Contact: Pastor	Churches, Parochial Schools, High Schools
Clubs	Board of Directors; Contact: Club Manager	Golf, yatching, swimming, tennis, riding, skiing, mixed sports (the family club)
Cultural	Board of Directors; Contact: Manager, Board Member	Museums, Music Schools, Concert Halls, Theaters, Community Centers

PRIVATE OWNER (SINGLE OR CORPORATE)		
Banks	President, Board of Directors; Recommendations for selection at times by a designated officer. Contact: President, Vice President	Banks, Office Buildings
Entertainment	Owner of establishment; Contact: Owner or Manager	Motion picture theaters, Bowling, skating, and swimming facilities, arenas
Commerce	Board of Directors, President; Contact: Property Manager	Office Buildings, Business and Professional
Industry	President of Company, Board of Directors. Contact: President	Industrial, Manufacturing and Processing Plants
Sales & Services	Owner of establishment; Contact: Properties Manager	Stores, Shopping Centers, Service establishments, Hotels, etc.

chapter 5

What and How to Copy —
These Are the Questions

ONE OF THE problems plaguing more architects than are willing to admit it is that of copying and imitating ideas from other architects. Not to copy is next to impossible. To copy from poor models is a heavy retardant on one's business. To recognize, however, the good model and to re-create from it through catalysis, as a new expression and furtherance of the original thought, is one of the great assets of the effective architect. An architect must accept the premise that he cannot escape the influence of the work of other architects. Most architectural designs are the continuance of a previous thought. For architecture to advance at an intelligent pace, this must be so. If every building were a new, unrelated thought we would have chaos.

But advance must not lose itself in wasteful dead-end exploits of fashion following. The architect whose designs are, by virtue of his ability to master the art of copying, beyond temporary fashion accomplishes two significant tasks: every one of his buildings is a stepping-stone in the stair of acclaim, and the increase of useful life and value of his buildings is one of the most convincing selling points.

This chapter illuminates the design modes which are fashion, then outlines the key thoughts of copying, followed by rules by which the good model is recognized and selected, and concludes with adaptation techniques.

The Value of a Building

The value of a building is of prime significance to the owner. Therefore the value should relate to the building's cost as favorably as possible. Obviously, the relation increases in favor of value if a building:

  a) remains pleasing in appearance, that is, outclasses fashion-following contemporaries,
  b) needs little maintenance, retaining its stability and general good quality,
  c) is internally sufficiently flexible to permit periodic changes to accommodate variations of function.

While internal planning and choice of lasting materials may not always be fully controllable by the architect, the exterior appearance is indeed subject to his master minding. No other attribute determines the length of life quite so much; the desirability of a building is directly proportional to its appearance. When the desirability wanes, the building's value declines with it. As the decline reaches the low point, it must either be remodeled or replaced. Of greatest interest is how soon that point is reached.

Hit Parade in Stone

There is a story that a certain business-minded glazier, whenever low on work, sent his apprentice down the various streets and had him, with the aid of well-aimed stones, break as many windows as possible. The good glazier followed a few blocks behind to offer the valued services of his trade and, with the gratefulness of the homeowners, reglazed many broken pieces.

While an architect can't go down the street knocking down buildings so he can replace them, many might just as well have done so. In the many designs of short-lived fashion, some architects have implanted the time bomb of demolition, set to go off when newer fashions have dated his previous work. The architect of such buildings is then labeled old-fashioned or considered an unable designer. The owner, if asked why he is of that opinion, has one simple answer: his building was built not very long ago but already looks old compared to others.

As a typical example: A few years ago, the administration of a high school system decided to replace a large three-story classroom building on one of their main campuses. The building was 30 years old. By chance I conversed with the architect about it. He made the statement, typical of the situation, "I don't know why they have to tear it down – it was a good building." I did not have the heart to tell him why. A few weeks earlier I was invited to discuss the possibility of repair and remodeling. Inflexible with its 16' x 16' bays of mediocre structural strength and ugly as could be on inside and out, it was perfectly senseless. The architect was, of course, not commissioned to design the replacement structure.

The sobering facts are that there are countless outdated office buildings, apartments, stores, schools, institutions, yes, even churches, from one end of the country to the other, which are now being demolished, or will be in the next three decades – broken out of the system like old, ugly teeth. Why? Because the day has come when they have finally gone off the hit parade. The architect who designed them followed the temporary fashions; those coming thereafter did likewise. By necessity did these older ones sink into oblivion with the emergence of the "latest."

Perhaps the most striking of all examples are the many city centers which must periodically undergo complete rebuilding, since their layout and appearance alienate them from modern society's needs. Nowhere can the effective architect point as a better proof, when he proposes good architecture and planning to his client.

Fashion Without Models

Fashion in architecture is not at all obvious to many architects. In fact, until one has become aware of it, the cause of many problems remains a mystery. The ability to discover comes only through disciplined self-education (it would be a great error to believe that schools of architecture only teach "absolutes") and keen observation. The question why one's building of a few years ago now looks a bit dull and unattractive is a very important question for the architect. The discovery that one followed a fashion rather than a model is a significant turning point.

To isolate this point I will outline five major fashions architecture has undergone in roughly the last two decades. Four can be attributed to pure momentary fancy, since they are devoid of logical precedent or significant following. The fifth is what I have called the 28th echo of classicism. Not one contained a single new thought or was based on logical design – neither could such postulates as "form follows function" or "organic architecture" be made applicable.

For example, there was a sudden emergence of the concrete "folded plate" roof. The system has a certain appeal of structural ingenuity to be sure, but it invaded many a building, whether logical or not. Eventually the application became absurd when it was imitated with other materials. There were, and will be, buildings for which the folded plate is well suited, but only those buildings will enjoy a longer life and have greater value to their owners. (See Fig. 5.1.)

Then there is the 28th echo, another form of rebirth of colonnaded and entablatured styles. The rebirth has been greatly intensified in the past years and may continue for a while yet. While more appealing than current fashion to most laymen, the 28th echo (not the classic models) has serious shortcomings. The reason is that classic architecture is not really taught any more as an architectural design discipline but rather as historic curiosity. The majority of designers have therefore no idea what they are doing when attempting to employ classical principles. Consequently, in the process of imitation forms become meaningless and crude, and violate harmonious proportions. While this fashion could well exist with contemporary thought, the necessary skill for its catalysis is lacking. If the catalysis were successful, the fashion could become a rather appealing design mode. (See Figs. 5.2 and 5.3.)

Surprisingly, the more temporal fashions are the result of a sort of architects' incest: "styles" discovered and promulgated through awards by architectural jurors. For example, the design mode of the Engineering Science Center at the University of Colorado at Boulder was, through the winning of an award, suddenly thrust into prominence. (See Fig. 5.4.)

Fig. 5.1 The Folded Plate. There seemed to be no other possible way to roof any building except through folded plates.

It has subsequently been copied for all conceivable and inconceivable functions — dormitories, schools of all kinds, houses of course, churches, hospitals. Most copies were monuments to the designer's limits, oblivious of the needs of the owner.

Then there is a style of sharp rectilinear shapes, achieved mostly with masonry and brick, sometimes softened with slightly rounded building corners and the liberal use of fluted concrete. Obviously, many an architect seems to find great security in its framework. (See Fig. 5.5.)

There is hardly a city in this country in which these forms are not found in the newer buildings. The design mode does unfortunately contain all the elements of fashion and will, when expired, be eradicated as fervently as the buildings of the 20's. (See Fig. 5.6.)

The quite recent fashion is the "mansard" style. Ripped indescriminately off the attic floor of multi-storied living-buildings of uncertain vintage, this derivation in the search for something new is not only devoid of logic but is marked by ugliness. (See Fig. 5.7.)

While confined first to low-rise commercial buildings, it is now the trademark of many houses and has finally infected larger buildings not in the least suited for this fad.

To conclude the illumination of what are faddish styles, the writer leaves it to the reader to reflect on "habitat after '67".

Fig. 5.2   Classicistic rebirth: The 28th Echo. This happens to be a cosmetic factory. The form apparently follows any function.

Modularism

For the effective architect, the full implications of the modular and, synonymously, the strictly homogenous architecture is something worthy of considerable thought. Unfortunately, the immediate results (I speak here of perhaps a dozen years) are often appealing but the almost preclusive inflexibility of the system imposes grave restrictions for the future. Most of all, the original style, once continued beyond the initial stage, soon forms an unbreakable pattern which right or wrong must be followed. (See Fig. 5.8.)

Some years ago I was commissioned to continue the work on a new junior college. The original, consisting of about eight buildings, was not only modular in design but also homogenous. For the first larger expansion program the client was already forced into a dilemma. Should he continue the same style and module, thus furthering complete rigidity and perpetuation of an expensive construction (the original ran 12% over the budget), or should he break free, clearly isolating the original campus as a momentary fashion, possibly even error?

My client had no conception that these problems even existed, let alone demanded solutions. In fact he was deeply irritated that he should have had such misguidance by

Fig. 5.3 The mansard temple, a composite fashion indiscriminately eclectic.

Fig. 5.4 Engineering Center, University of Colorado. It set the fashion for virtually everything.

University of Colorado Photo

Fig. 5.5 New City Hall, Boston. He who refuses to design inverted matchbox pyramids will never win an architect's award. In 1970 this reached the top of the hit parade.

my predecessor, in particular, since it looked all so pleasant until the day of expansion arrived. The solution finally accepted by all was a compromise. However, the initial error kept irritated and perplexed minds active for some time. The first architect has not, to this day, designed another building on that campus.

The Art of Copying

To copy effectively, four basic processes must be recognized: (a) the correct attitude toward copying; (b) recognition of the worthwhile model; (c) selection of the best suited model; and, (d) adaptation and refinement for one's new design.

The Correct Attitude

The effective architect must be aware of an elemental aspect of copying, without which culture could not evolve. Mankind's knowledge and cultural possessions all are based on orderly evolution. It is a necessary process for the development and refinement of ideas and concepts. If every generation started culture anew, man would never be further from his primitive ignorance than one life span. Architects, like anyone else,

Fig. 5.6 Apartment, office building, school? The function always follows form. A definite refinement of the fashion.

Fig. 5.7 Another age, a different City Hall. Barely 2 years later than Boston – the hit parade must go on.

Fig. 5.8 A School of Medicine, Duke University. The fashion is frozen since the initial module. Too far the other way, it is restrictive and very costly.

simply cannot do more than improve on each other's ideas and accomplishments. Only once in a great while is a truly new thought introduced, by a genius. While one in 100,000 architects offers the new thought, 99,999 must subsequently refine it. In the process of refinement many an ingenious detail will evolve, eventually enriching the new thought into a perfected style.

One of the characteristics of the ineffective architect is his fear of being considered uncreative. "Uncreative" to him means "not original." The inefficiency arises from the fact that he is copying, in fact must do so, but simultaneously persuading himself that he is indeed original.

There he stands, on the threshold of impending greatness. He will now design a new building, beautiful and original beyond his own (and everyone else's) wildest dreams. So he enters seclusion to free his mind to create. There he wrestles with his most powerful emotions, (and glances through architectural magazines), to reappear again, serene and victorious: he has "created" a new building. Except, that it was all self-deception. He knew at the beginning he would not really create anything new. The only issue he wrestled with was his own ego; he had to convince himself that he did not copy. Because he was impressed with that building of so-and-so, making a few little changes — for a different function anyway — brought his ego back into shape. Once more he successfully suppressed his conscience. I have observed so many architects during this process that I have come to recognize it as a professional character flaw.

This architect is ineffective, since he denies himself the true function of adding to the coherent substance of architectural culture, and, a more mundane consideration, also denies himself one of the most convincing selling points of his profession.

The effective architect must, as the first point of order, understand and accept the meaning of copying – that it is not a disgrace but inevitable, a good and useful necessity. It is absolutely necessary openly to seek out a work that can be admired and follow its lead. He neither steals nor is he mentally infertile. He must come to accept this concept or his sin will eventually make him a sad mimic.

Recognition of Good Models

The process is substantially a matter of maturity of one's own critical judgment. I will list some basic rules by which the validity of a good mode of design can be established.

Rule 1 is the congruency of the design with the principal function of a building. Examples of excellent congruency are the Senate and Chamber of Deputies of the National Congress of Brasilia (Niemeyer) (Fig. 5.11). Then there is the U.S. Embassy at New Delhi (E. D. Stone) (Fig. 5.10), and similar in nature, the President's Palace at Brasilia (Niemeyer). Other examples are the Sports Palazzi at Rome (Nervi); the Lakeshore Apartments (Mies van der Rohe); the Dulles Airport (Saarinen) (Fig. 5.9) or, one of the many isolated works of genius, the tetrahedron-shaped church of Hyvinkaa (Ruusjvouri), Finland (Figs. 5.12 and 5.13).

Of course the great historic structures are examples par excellence, in particular the cruciform Gothic church, or more technical structures like an aqueduct. The outstanding characteristic of these examples is the complete agreement between shape and function, never submitting to capriciousness or fancy.

Rule 2 inquires into the logic of the structural system and material used. Typical for the good model is that both are complementary to the shape. The solutions are elegant and not forced, economical in terms of quantity. There is restraint and discipline in the materials used. The material does things peculiar to its own characteristics and is never used to imitate other materials. The good model observes the intrinsic nature of materials.

Rule 3 concerns itself with, what I will call, the soul of the structure – the infusion of the designer's spirit, emotion and creative power. The good model in which function, structural system and material are in harmony, also possesses the quality of beauty, the emission of noble and desirable attributes. While Rules 1 and 2 deal with matters of logic, Rule 3 embraces those aspects which render the building alive, humane, desirable and an object of enjoyment.

As a subordinate point, the surface character of materials becomes important. Is the scale of values, the range from raw concrete through plaster, tile, and wood paneling to marble and such highly developed surfaces as bas relief, correctly scaled?

The characteristics of the three rules are found in all good models. The good model is a single whole, not the combination of component thoughts. Never is a good model a plan over which a structure is engineered, a facade architected to, or an interior

Official Photograph Federal Aviation Agency

Fig. 5.9   Dulles International Airport. Matching the jet in grace and technical logic.

decorated into. An architect who is attracted to works of excellence of another architect should study his designs and analyze, yes, even subject to rigorous critique, such work.

Selection of the Model

The previous discussion has outlined how good models are recognized. Obviously most architects are attracted to at least one, but usually several, modes of design. From this stock the right model must be chosen for a given design.

For the selection, a series of mental steps is necessary to determine congruency of model and project in question. One must be sure what one's building is to express. That is not always clear. For example, who is to say what a physics building on a campus should be like to be identifiable with "physics," or a florist's store with "flowers"? To make the determination easier, one must attach further attributes, such as, "education, research, science" to "physics" and "display, selling, service, atmosphere" to "florist's store." Again, the physics building should, in its appearance at least, observe laws of statics as reduced to their simplest terms; it may show definite geometric shapes but all congruent with the laws of physics. The florist's store, on the other hand,

Courtesy of Edward Durell Stone

Fig. 5.10 United States Embassy, New Delhi, India. The architectural ambassador – the form expresses the function.

should attract people, should display the flowers in a most inviting manner, as a good drink should be served in a beautiful glass, thus increasing the desire for consumption. Therefore, the definition itself must become sufficiently precise to decide upon congruency of function. The model on the other hand must have expressed its own purpose equally well. It is, however, not necessary that functions of model and proposed project be the same.

It is, incidentally, taken for granted that the effective architect has a library covering historic and contemporary structures of note, permitting him an overview of the cultural heritage of architecture.

Adaptation

The final step, and the most significant one, is the adaptation of the model's mode of design to one's project. To begin with, the choice of material must be correct. I have found it to be best if the material of the model is used, if necessary with some modification. Material belongs to a style, a design mode. One must resist the temptation to make arbitrary choices – like a vaulted brick ceiling convincingly suspended from a

Courtesy Departmento de Turismo & Recreacao

Fig. 5.11 The Congress, Brasilia. The ultimate in functional logic: the dome and bowl as assembly halls. Also a magnificant sculptural harmony.

reinforced concrete system above. Materials are chosen not because one can do anything with them, but because they are the logical solution in terms of design, availability and climatic resistance.

The second step is the one in which the architect's skill comes to greatest expression: the refinement and furtherance of the model. Two points must be observed. First, no building is so similar that a direct transposition is practical or even feasible. Therefore the elements of the model's design are used as an example, not the design itself. Secondly, no design is so perfect that it should be perpetuated without variation or improvement. In history one finds, as a significant pattern, the tendency toward greater delicateness or lightness of members and refinements of proportions. This holds true today. If one's copy brings some elements peculiar to a design mode to greater prominence, it becomes a caricature of the original. The public's reaction to these caricatures is unrestrained; "Have you seen that awful looking thing?" or, "Wonder what they'll come up with next?" A sort of antithesis to the public's harsh judgments is the architectural award juries' verdicts hailing these caricatures as creations worthy of virtual idolatry.

Invariably successful will be a copy which respects scale, not only as a transposition

Matti Saanio, Rovaniemi, Finland

Fig. 5.12   The Church of Hyvinkaa. The Trinity symbolized.

but also as a further step in evolution. To state an abstract example, a brick has certain dimensions, regardless of the size of the building. If the design demands larger masses where brick becomes a veneer around elements obviously structural, its use requires the greatest caution if the scale, established by the brick as a unit, is not to be destroyed.

Finally, proportions, lines, curves, areas, the entire framework of harmonic unity and detail motifs of the original, should through catalysis be re-created by the new mind, by him who is capable of applying his good taste, critical judgment and re-creative skill to infuse into the building the elements of beauty, logic and sensibleness, thus elevating the copy from a mere act of imitative skill to a new work of art.

Matti Saanio, Rovaniemi, Finland

Fig. 5.13   Church of Hyvinkaa, Finland. The Trinity expressed within. A religious sculpture of perfection.

chapter 6

The Secrets of
the Profitable Office

A LAWYER FRIEND of mine once told me, "A case is not won through the brilliant cross examination in court, but through the arduous, exacting and most exhausting preparation in one's office." Translated for our profession: the architect does not make his money through splendid appearances in clubs and citizen committees or through learned talk, but by what he does in his office and how he does it.

The product of the architect's office is almost always nontypical. Yet much of the operation can be standardized. Procedures must, therefore, be subjected to the closest scrutiny so that efficient working patterns may be developed.

This chapter discusses the less obvious but economically significant aspects, like promotional cost, ideal office size and the elements of the Two-Man Team. In addition, project costs of a sampling of over 40 projects of varying sizes are compared to recommended fee schedules. Finally, stratagems to make "omnium-gatherum" projects profitable are listed.

A Job Meanders Through the Good-Old Office

If I consolidate my own experiences with those of the hundreds of draftsmen and architect friends of mine from all parts of the country in order to describe the typical American office, a quaint and perhaps historically curious pattern emerges. Let me qualify the preceding by saying that many enlightened firms operate on a more organized level; nonetheless there are those who are worse.

The scene is a drafting room with an allotment of 42 square feet per draftsman. The atmosphere is like a salt mine, the walls are cluttered with things of which not even the oldest staff member can remember the origin. A few pinned up wisecracks and nudes freshen up the environment. Seniority is strictly maintained and everybody knows his place.

The chief draftsman is no better an architect than the boss; the firm either doesn't design (which is the case most of the time) or, in critical instances, relies on the talents of a young graduate. There are several trusty team captains who know where and what to trace and how to put a job together. The strata below consist of the "draughtsmen," and then there is the junior level — where the existence in the twilight of architecture alternates between floor sweeping, bordering of sheets and perhaps cupboard details.

The boss brings in some sketches, hieroglyphic in appearance and often with a touch of solid dilettantism: the definition of the project as arrived at between himself and the client the evening before. These graphic fragments are then handed to the chief draftsman (or the design boy) with equally poor oral explanation. If the boss is the progressive type, the designer is supposed to get the information he needs or, as we say nowadays, is encouraged to engage in the necessary research. But if the boss is old-fashioned, an odd and bizarre trial-and-error guessing game proceeds until the building has been beaten into some shape — a shape acceptable to the boss, the trusty structural engineer and, of course, the client.

That kind of boss had only time to look at the sketches at five minutes to quitting time, or when he as usual came back in the evening. (As a habitual overtimer, he never got anything done during the day.) In the intervening days of waiting, an unhappy designer chewed through several pencils and filled rolls of "thin" out of sheer boredom.

This boss, being successful only because he was there before most other architects, had never learned how to delegate responsibility. He made all the mediocre decisions himself. His tried and proven spec never changed and would still tell the Gold Bond people how to slack lime, the painters how to grain doors, and almost everybody what kind of tools to use.

Interestingly, this boss made surprisingly little profit, was fully content to work ten to twelve hours per day, and in many cases saw no vacation for years. His personal office was chaotic: he was surrounded by towering stacks of magazines, unopened mail, brochures, letters, notices, pieces and bits of blueprints, samples and so on. If he complained of too much work he did so with pride, acknowledged by the staff with sweet-sour smiles. His personal efficiency was extremely low. The only reason he can exist at all is his innumerable connections and dependable friends. His working drawings fared best. Extensive cribbing from past jobs eliminated all possible danger of experimentation. Perhaps his only laudable act was managing to put a passably solid building together.

The days of these offices are coming to an end. The sophisticated and technological society of our age begins to demand a better performance. Simultaneously, competition is becoming keener. Therefore, a highly efficient office is essential if an architect wishes to exist and grow. The steps to efficiency are self-analysis and alignment of organization.

Cost Records

The key is the keeping of accurate cost records. These records are only of value if they are relatable to each and every project, and subdivided into the following major phases:

     a) Promotion
     b) Design
     c) Working Drawings
     d) Supervision

Other major phases are engineering fees and the applicable portion of general operations.

Timekeeping must start with the principal of the firm because he is usually the most costly entity of the enterprise. Too many architects believe that they, as owners, are part of the overhead and that a multiplier related to the production staff will take care of their existence. If this principal, upon examination of his own time records, discovers that the best part of his time went into administrative duties of the office, and the remainder into client contacts, he would do well to analyze the effectiveness of his administrative work as related to that of client contacts and the acquisition of commissions. In all likelihood he will find that a well-paid business manager could take care of 95% of the administrative duties, allowing him to devote his entire time to client contacts. Obviously, the latter is of a higher degree of difficulty and consequently has a higher yield.

On the other hand, if an attempt at timekeeping shows his activities to be so diversified as to make timekeeping a downright annoyance, he should more than ever discipline himself and account for his time and action, since his own performance is in all likelihood quite inefficient.

Timekeeping by the principal may also indicate the general direction in which the business is going, or the direction in which it could be led. For example, in most newer offices promotional time is directly related to the work volume. As an office grows, the time may come when the principal's entire efforts have to go into client contacts. At that point he ceases to be an architect and becomes businessman. If then, for example, he is a very good designer, the direction is inefficient since selling is easier than designing.

Much consolation is being offered from efficiency experts to the executive who utters the common complaint, "I hardly get anything done any more." I, for one, offer no consolation. This executive has simply lost track of his actions. The most inefficient position in which many a principal appears to find himself is that of the petty administrator. To free one's self from the avalanche of daily small tasks, phone calls, trivialities and time wasters, one must regroup tasks into blocks. This involves delegation of responsibility to someone else. For example, no principal should keep his fingers in the daily routine of supervision if his office has a field inspector. Telephone calls relating to supervision should be refused and turned over to the field man. The same applies to shop prints, monthly cost accounting, and general field correspondence. The field is one block.

Likewise, purchasing and maintenance of office supplies, bookkeeping, printing and duplicating, contracts and billing, insurances, donations, conventions, office cars, the payroll, and so on, all with their many daily details can consume a good percentage of the principal's day unless they are ordered into routine blocks and delegated. A principal who is unable to do so has come to a standstill.

Cost records are extremely useful, but only if they are frequently analyzed and correctly interpreted. It must be recognized that costs are not always relatable to a fee schedule (and its fractional progress payments), since most architects have their own standards of work quantity within the various phases.

Some of the most obvious occurrences are:

a) One or more phases, like design and supervision, were extremely costly: the choice of designer may have been a bad one, or the program poorly written; or the construction presented unexpected difficulties due to errors in plans.

b) All phases are over the fee: most probably the fee was too low since it is unlikely that all participants "blundered" simultaneously.

c) Excessive profits were made: there is every reason for suspicion that the quality was neglected. (Incidentally, this does happen!)

The real value of analysis and interpretation is feed-back into the organization, to correct and refine procedure that both quality of work and profits may increase.

Overhead

One of the great difficulties in the determination of the overhead is the variableness of what it should include.

What must be included as basic is simple enough: all operational cost with the exception of production staff salaries and engineering fees. (An immediate ambiguity is the typing of specifications by the secretary.)

Debatable remains the principal's salary and profit.

Let it be assumed that the portion of the principal's salary which is attributable to promotion should be added to overhead. What is left then is profit, which should be the difference between all operational costs plus overhead and the fee actually received. To compute a multiplier per hourly rate for either principal or production staff is then routine arithmetic.

If, on the other hand, no salary for the principal exists, and his income is simply equal to all profit, a multiplier can become very misleading and even indeterminable, should it serve as a basis for an hourly rate. The determination of the hourly rate should be made from extensive and accurate records to avoid self-delusion.

Promotional Costs

Because of the increasing number of architectural offices, the necessity to go out and promote is becoming inevitable. The cost of promotion must, of course, be absorbed and should not necessarily consume too much of one's profits. This dictates a highly effective form of promotion as outlined previously. It also presupposes greater efficiency in all other work phases, since the additional cost must be regained in the operation.

Promotional costs can, of course, get out of hand unless they are closely observed and related to some reasonable standard. I have, based on many records, established an empirical guideline which shows that promotional costs may broadly vary from 1/200th to 1/2000th of the cost of a project. The distribution of the ratios is represented in the graph of Fig. 6.1.

In the construction of a graph illustrating promotional costs, it is perfectly correct also to include projects which went to other firms or simply failed to materialize for some reason or another, but there should be a reasonable certainty that nothing more could have been done in the course of promoting it. Typical, for example, are the interviews of building committees and their eventual decisions (which may be likened to the rolling of dice).

While the graph in Fig. 6.1 represents the range which I consider tolerable, it should not be concluded that it states inexorable limits. Not infrequently a project, especially

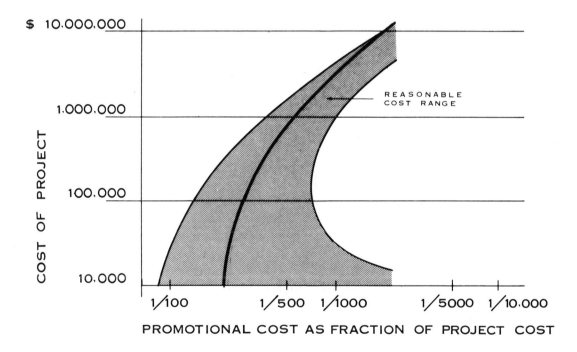

Fig. 6.1 Promotion Cost. This graph illustrates the average cost of promotion, which lies between 1/200th and 1/2000th of the project cost in the range between $10,000. and $10,000,000. of project cost. The costs are those applied directly against specific projects, but not including general promotion, like brochures, firm image, listing, etc. Included are salaries, travel, entertainment, research and preparation. As an example, to promote a $500,000. project, cost should lie (between $660. and $2300.) at $1250. The majority of this amount is due to principal's time.

of the "omnium-gatherum" kind, is the beginning of much more for which promotional cost is reduced to a mere trifle. In such instances, promotional cost for the first hundred thousand may well be 1/100th, but for the next million be down to 1/10,000th. I should hasten to say that an attempt to avoid any loss at all is prudent nevertheless.

Along the same line, the ratio of work obtained to work lost varies greatly. It is a most interesting figure every office should establish for themselves. Over the years, I have found that I must pursue at least five times the volume I will eventually be commissioned for. I have furthermore observed that the ratio decreases as the volume increases. This corresponds with the fact that firms with a very small work volume, say less than one million per year, have proportionately higher promotional costs than those with volumes of five million and up.

Promoting While the Office Is Busy

An orderly growth can only be attained if the work coming in does so in linear, non-erratic fashion. Most architects make the natural error of ignoring the search for further commissions when they have good projects on the board. They engage only in promoting work when they have none, or are about to run out. The importance of promotion, in particular when there is plenty of work in the office, cannot be overstressed. Otherwise, the operation becomes erratic, where slack periods consume profits and cause staff turnovers, and, on the other hand, heavy loads endanger completion schedules and quality. I have found it to be a good rule to get into action for new work as soon as any project has had preliminary approval.

What Size Office Is Best?

Rodin did not have a staff where one was responsible for the legs, another for arms, and so on. He not only decided upon expression, mood, pose and the choice of material but he also sculptured legs, arms, and so on. That, in my opinion, is the ideal, directly translatable into architecture: one master who is personally engaged in the artistic, technological and constructional spheres of every building. Attached to this master may be one or more assistants and apprentices.

Our society is not so much interested in masterworks as it is in quantity and speed. Although this is regrettable, the effective architect must adapt himself to the point of reasonable compromise.

The ideal office of our time is one which centers around a principal or leader who should, like a conductor of a symphony orchestra, be thoroughly familiar with all facets of the act: design, working drawings, client relationships, business administration, field work and many more. But most of all, he should be the designer. Not only is this psychologically preferable, it also places him at the helm: he wholly controls, influences and guides the enterprise in its most decisive professional facet.

This office should be large enough to execute projects up to 15,000,000 cubic feet per year, something which can be accomplished with a staff of 12 to 15. The reader should know that a project as large as 10,000,000 cubic feet makes the nation's largest offices, with staffs of many hundred people, anxious to secure it. Any office that can execute this kind of volume is big league and can talk on even terms with anybody.

While there are many purely organizational reasons which make the 2 to 15 people office the most desirable, the chief advantage lies in the keynote of individualism, so essential in architecture. Larger firms are forced eventually to follow a flat scheme. Also, the smaller firm can place responsibility upon its work, whereas the larger firm must shift it more towards its continued existence. What should be individual creation is likely to become statistical output.

Last, though not least, the personal incomes of a master and his staff members may well exceed those of all but the very highest executives of the larger firms. In addition life is a bit easier, less strained, providing a more conducive atmosphere for architecture and architects. Therefore, the ideal office of our time is predicated on the qualitative and quantitative limits of creativeness of the master designer who, if at all possible, should be the principal of the firm.

The Two-Man Team

Following this axiom, some years ago I discarded conventional clichés and instituted in my office the Two-Man Team, of which I am one member and one of my staff the other. Several such teams exist in parallel. Since I originate most designs, the limit of the office's capacity lies in my ability to design. That, however, is not absolutely rigid, since the completeness of design can be fairly flexible. Completeness may vary with the other team member's design ability or his comprehension of my thoughts, or the complexity of the project.

The result of the system is that: (a) the second team member enjoys a close personal relationship with his principal; (b) nothing else will acquaint him with the principal's thinking as thoroughly; (c) the second team member knows the project most intimately, making him far more efficient in the preparation of drawings than if several draftsmen were attached to the traditional team captain; and (d) the second member can act as understudy in client-architect conferences, something which is extremely gratifying!

What happens if the project is very large and drawings must be completed in a short time? First of all, the efficiency of the team member is usually such that he can complete working drawings in one-third of the time, since he need not instruct or supervise others, and because he no longer experiences the ruinous periods of standstill caused by indecisiveness of his boss. Therefore, if the projects are below the two to three million cubic feet level, the speed of completion is nearly the same as the traditional system, but most of all it comfortably matches the speed of the consulting engineers in their work. Furthermore, the project can be broken down into individual buildings or other appropriate quantities and then distributed over two or more Two-Man Teams. It requires, of course, a bit more supervisory attendance by the principal architect, which he should give at least for larger projects.

The Pattern of Major Organizational Functions

An organizational feature which has significantly improved the quality and reliability of the contract documents is that specifications are always written by someone outside the particular team. (I consider the so-called "Specwriter," be he consultant or staff, not the ideal solution since the experience base is eventually too narrow to produce a good legal, technical and also practical specification.) In the same spirit, estimates are made by an "unbiased" staff member.

One of the most costly, nerve-wracking and time-consuming aspects in the preparation of most drawings is the picking up of tag ends, the touching up here and there, the little change that goes through twenty sheets, the correction of some minor dimensional disorder, two or three score of still missing details, and so on. While the method of the Two-Man Team reduces these occurrences at the outset, I have introduced a simple device by which these incompletions are properly noted and taken care of. As the drawings near completion, a "rider" checklist is attached to each drawing, containing a running record of all the missing items, corrections, changes, etc. If a change affects six out of nine sheets, the six riders of the respective sheets will simultaneously receive an entry. Thus chance discoveries are virtually absent.

I have found it to be most effective to treat and operate supervision and general office administration as autonomous departments. Both are complex, yet routine areas of activity but need not be part of the principal's work.

Project Cost

As I mentioned previously, not only the most important but also the most revealing thing in one's office is an accurate cost record of projects. Since the beginning of my firm, I have kept and collected cost records of nearly all projects and, for the purpose of fee verification, compared them to the recommended schedules of the American Institute of Architects. The results are represented in Fig. 6.2.

The significance of this curve is that, all things equal, projects below 200,000 cubic feet have a loss potential if fees as recommended by the American Institute of Architects are applied. Firms that have their CG in work of this size are likely to suffer a lower income. They cannot gain sufficient profit to prepare themselves to obtain a commission for a more profitable and larger project, and are forced to continue at a substandard income from poorly paid small projects. Firms, on the other hand, with a good variety of projects often ignore the loss in smaller ones because the overall picture looks good. Their organizations could be much more efficient if such losses were halted and efforts made to bring such work into the profit sphere.

It is not necessary that small projects automatically spell smaller profits. The employment of several strategies does provide the basis for a profitable job; from there on, close surveillance is necessary to keep the project on schedule. The best strategies are the following:

Obtain
a) The highest possible fee at the very outset. (I have dealt with this subject in Chapter 3, Fee.)
b) An understanding of how many meetings the architect must attend with the client or the committee.

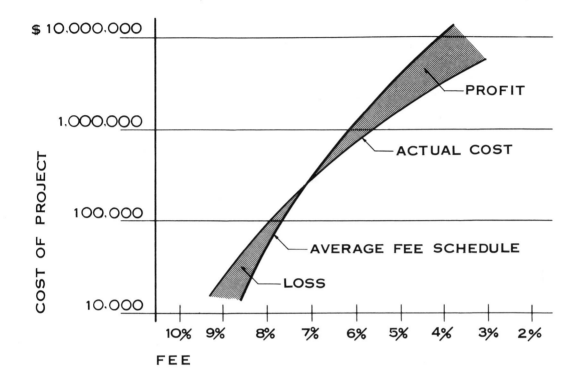

Fig. 6.2 Cost vs. General Fee. The graph shows the potential loss and profit ranges for architectural consulting services related to project cost, as derived by equalizing and plotting a number of projects. Many would be outside this range, since fees did not always correspond with the recommended schedule.

c) Exclusion of a rendering from the standard basic services. I suggest the modification to a black and white line perspective in lieu thereof.
d) A definite program. Time spent here is best applied.

Other considerations are:

e) Simple design — a minimum of preliminary drawings.
f) The structure should be firmed up in the earliest possible stage, preferably before interior or exterior decorating is begun.
g) Working drawings traced from preliminaries.
h) Most specifications on drawings themselves.
i) Simplified specifications — all verbiage deleted.
j) Mechanical, plumbing and electrical systems and specifications equally brief and definitive.
k) Good estimates — always conservative.
l) Obtaining of client's written approval for each phase.

m) Supervision only when and where necessary. All other visits should be avoided.
n) Paperwork held to a minimum.

The reader will have noticed the substance of these strategies: an artificially elevated fee and the least waste motion in the execution of the work. Of course, it would be easier all around if fees were better adjusted to the work necessary, but regrettably they are not. Hence, rather than reducing one's income, a systematic working mode is the most intelligent answer.

chapter 7

The Useful Consultant and How to Make Him So

WHEN THE AIR conditioning doesn't work, the client calls the architect, not the mechanical engineer. When a vicious crack in a structural member has occurred, a red-faced architect must answer. Why was a similar building so much more graceful and also cost less? These and hundreds of issues evolve around the architect's consultants.

This chapter provides a guide for selecting the best consultants and controlling them once engaged. It concludes with a description of the less common consultants, and when to employ them.

The Typical Case

In the practice of architecture, one of the most difficult things to predict is the quality of the consultant's work. One is again and again compelled to ponder the same questions: is it really the best solution? How well will it work? Is the design within the budget?

Some years ago, I designed a scalloped, thin shell of about 150 feet diameter for a church group. The design was orderly, employing elementary curves. A model was constructed and everybody was pleased with its graceful shape. I proceeded to select for the project a structural engineer who was said to be the most experienced. During the structural calculations, the engineer insisted it was necessary to make increasingly significant changes. When the drawings and calculations were completed, the design had lost its gracefulness, and was ugly and bulky. Its costs would obviously exceed the budget. While I was quite unhappy about this, I knew I had chosen the wrong man. The fee for the project barely covered the already runaway production costs; therefore, to engage another engineer was out of the question.

As expected, the bids were well over the budget. An analysis of the figures given to me by the low bidder clearly showed the shell as solely responsible for the excess. I attempted to place the responsibility in the engineer's hands, but, of course, it did not solve the problem. In fact, the only answer was to have the shell redesigned by someone else.

Most fortunately the client, who was kept fully informed, not only agreed to a redesign but to assume the cost incurred, providing the reduction in the cost of construction would exceed the cost of redesign by a good margin. The shell was then structurally redesigned and also re-bid. The final cost reduction amounted to fifteen times the engineer's fee! And, the shell had recovered its original gracefulness.

How could I have avoided this string of disagreeable occurrences? There is no simple answer. Primarily, the selection of a consulting engineer would have required far greater care. At the first instance of disagreement, I should have evaluated the point at issue in the light of the future. The change to another engineer could have been made at that time with little money lost. But I let the situation worsen itself until it was too late. The fact that the project was saved was due in large part to luck. However, the lesson was profound. I have since taken greater care in the selection of engineers.

Reasons for Commissions

Before the architect engages any consultant, he should take greatest care to analyze the reasons why he is choosing this man or firm in particular, to perform the professional services. In the subsequent analysis, the positive and negative aspects are weighed in a thorough manner, predicting to the best of one's ability the coming performance of the consultant.

I should like to make a definite point here: no consultant, no matter how well he has performed in the past, should be re-engaged without this prior inquiry into his qualifications for the new project.

The first point in question is his suitability. For example, does the project call for the consultant's innovative thinking, originality and possibly even daring? If so, has the consultant exhibited such abilities elsewhere? Or, is extreme economy the principal requirement? Will the consultant then devote his undivided interest to find the most elegant and economic solution? Will he analyze alternative systems and prepare valid estimates? Is the project of critical nature with regard to mechanics of material, thermal movement, or connections for complex framing details, all demanding of him great thoroughness? Has he demonstrated just such abilities in his professional performance, through exact drawings, flawless calculations and specifications? In summary, is his mode of operation complementary to the project?

A second aspect, often decisive, is his competence as specialist. The reasons for choosing a specialist are twofold: his knowledge shall accrue to the benefit of the project, technically and economically, but shall also enhance the architect's status as the responsible creator. Let me clarify this point to avoid any misunderstanding: just as an incompetent consultant will lessen the architect's image before his clients, so does his proficiency elevate it. A typical case is the following. I had for many years observed that one of my colleagues did not use post-tensioning systems, even though his structures were becoming clumsier and more expensive compared to contemporary projects of other architects. In answer to my question he replied, "My structural engineer does not believe in post-tensioning." The truth of the matter was that the structural engineer had hardly any experience. After having virtually lost one client and made many others raise their eyebrows, my colleague finally put a specialist with experience in post-tensioning to work. Of course, his designs and image instantly improved.

Another colleague of mine "swore" by steel. All went relatively well until he designed a project to be built in a typical non-steel area. Not only did the cost of his work become outlandish, but strange things began to happen within the building itself. A good consulting engineer should, in this case, have advised him of the best structural solution. That, too, is the sign of the experienced specialist. Just as the architect is expected to advise his client to his greatest benefit, so should the consultant advise the architect.

Another aspect is his capacity to meet deadlines. Strangely enough, the number of engineers and draftsmen in the consultant's employ seems to have no bearing at all on his ability to perform on time. I have seen a two-man office of a mechanical consultant miss a completion date by only two weeks on a fairly good-sized project, yet one with 75 employees, for a nearly identical building, miss by three weeks. The real difference, however, lay in the explanations for the delay! The small office was apologetic, the large one rude and uncivil. The significant factor, therefore, is not so much the size of the consultant's staff as his work load. Before a commitment is made, his ability to meet schedules should be ascertained.

Often architects hire consultants because they charge a fee lower than others. The effective architect simply doesn't do that. Anyone who does is behaving like the client who employs the architect with the lowest bid regardless of other considerations. On the other hand, fees should be matched to the work involved and are therefore, in all fairness, subject to negotiations, but only after the consultant has been commissioned and not before.

Quite frequently, a motivating cause for the engagement of a consultant is moral obligation. For example, an engineer may have performed well on a small, thankless job and the architect feels obligated to him. Or perhaps a project turned out to be a complete dud where everybody lost, including the engineers. A logical way to compensate then is to give him other projects. The reason is a good one, but his competence for the project should be established, otherwise the favor may lead to misperformance which will only worsen the strained relationship.

Creating Natural Competition

Just like architects who enjoy the continued confidence of one client, consulting engineers in a similar position seem to acquire a decided tendency toward staleness, inaccuracies and liberties such as missing deadlines. Of these three adverse characteristics, staleness is the most serious fault since it encroaches on the substance of the architect's work. It is not simple to find counter-measures, especially since professional staleness is difficult to recognize. It is like a slowly acting disease, with very subtle symptoms. Often the staleness has progressed so far that only disaster will awaken the architect. Disaster may be quite simply the sudden loss of one or several commissions. There could be of course many reasons for such a loss. Nevertheless, it is a strong indicator that a pillar of our society has been shaken: that of competition.

I can recommend to my colleagues a few relatively simple but quite radical steps by which the deterioration of consultants can be avoided. The substance of these is to keep him on his toes, never to let him get the impression that every job is automatically committed to him. Of these steps, the first is to engage only those consultants who also work for one's biggest competitors. In that way one benefits in a second-hand manner from the obvious success of those colleagues.

Step two is to encourage one's consultant to seek commissions from other, but only successful, colleagues.

Step three is to maintain a choice of at least two consultants for each project, and to alternate frequently. This is the only language, loud and clear, which is understood. The results are most gratifying in terms of effort and performance.

Step four is psychologically necessary: let the consultant at least ask for the commission. Never hand it to him on a silver platter, even if he is the obvious choice. In this manner a natural competition can be maintained which will serve the architect, his building and the client.

Contracts with Consultants

I suppose we architects all tend to make the same mistake at least twice. First, we are inviting trouble by our tardiness in getting a contract with our client, and then we turn right around and commission a consultant for the performance of a highly responsible and complex piece of work with less than a handshake. We do this because the amount of work to be done by consultants has through practice been so well established that in the majority of cases nothing goes wrong. Even so, recommendable it is not. If there is to be a handshake agreement only, at least one point should be agreed upon — the fee. And as stated previously, it is entirely correct to determine the fee for each project anew. If no formal contract is entered into, the architect should request from the consultant a letter agreement which states the terms of the following four basic elements:

  a) The services to be rendered should be listed in headings, such as the analysis of alternative designs or systems, the preparation of working drawings, specifications, calculations and the checking of shop drawings. If applicable, supervision should be included.
  b) The fee should be stated. I recommend most strongly that at least 20% of the consultant's fee be withheld until the project is complete.
  c) An understanding with regard to budget, adherence thereto, and the responsibility of making post-bid alterations is very important.

d) Finally a very important issue is time schedules. These too should be clear and acknowledged.

For larger projects and even more with larger engineering firms, carefully drafted instruments are entirely in order. Too much can go wrong for which there should be clear provisions if law suits are to be avoided.

How to Work with a New Consultant

Once the consulting engineer has been engaged and begins work for the first time, the keyword for the architect is caution. The least expensive things are words; the most expensive, construction wages and materials. Therefore, to get to the optimum solution, extensive technical discussions, during which the engineer displays his talents and learns the architect's desires, are most advisable.

There should at all times be adequate correspondence, recording all significant technical decisions. Quite often architects tend to write extensive minutes of meetings. I consider this a waste of time — what matters is the decision, not the argument leading to it.

Furthermore, it is a useful practice to request frequent estimates of the work. In my nearly twenty years as a practicing architect I have learned one thing about engineers: their estimates should never be fully trusted. It is one of the most infuriating things to see the mooncalf expression on the engineer's face when asked what this or that will cost, as though the question is totally absurd! Engineers seem rarely to re-analyze the cost of their work. I blame this on us, the architects. If we were less forgiving about low estimates, engineers would take greater pains to seek the most efficient solution. Therefore, to make oneself a useful consultant, a certain hardness is necessary. How often it has happened that a very costly design could have been, with very little more thinking, arranged more simply and economically. The issue is quite important to the architect. It must always be borne in mind that every error in the plans is the architect's responsibility and an impairment to his reputation. An engineer's error can, therefore, and does quite frequently, endanger the architect's professional existence.

One of the riskiest things is to hire an engineer solely on the strength of a recommendation. He may be totally unsuitable for the project, or personalities may clash. I once made the error of engaging a large firm because a colleague recommended the people. My sole knowledge came from one lunch with the principal whom I never saw again. Instead, my staff soon was in bitter controversy with arrogant subordinates of the engineering firm who made us all feel as though we worked for them! Their design was anything but what we wanted. In spite of numerous warnings, the bids came in 70% over their own estimates. It took me months to repair the damage with my client.

When I speak of caution, I also refer to the frequent (and understandable) habit of passing out more work to a new consultant before the first project has proved to be functioning and, of course, has come reasonably within the budget. The effective architect should wait at least one year and observe closely how the structure behaves, and how the air conditioning, plumbing, electrical installations and specialty items function. If the consultant's work proves to be good and he has followed through actively, he deserves to be given further commissions.

Deadlines

One of the most irritating and destructive acts consultants seem to delight in committing is missing deadlines. Much in life depends upon time connections between people being observed. In construction, timing is crucial. What good does it do if when drawings are delivered to the architect's office three weeks late a sheepish apology is advanced? How is the architect to tell his client that the engineer is holding things up? He would thereby plainly admit his misjudgment in hiring him.

There are two ways in which to handle lateness. First, the effective architect should not let the situation develop to begin with. He must frequently inspect progress to assure and encourage adherence to schedules. Secondly, he should, once deadlines have been missed, give the next project to someone else. Both consultants must be told that this factor was the deciding one. For the new consultants it will serve as a very graphic deterrent. The least advisable tactic is to rave and rant, and then forget quickly. On the next project, the consultant will be late — only this time, with almost no concern over the consequences. To make him useful, therefore, consistency is necessary.

As a final thought, the architect must always be cognizant of the fact that it is the consultant who must suggest, whereas the architect is the one who decides. Consultants should propose the available alternatives. If they lack either the ability or imagination to do so, they are fairly useless. If challenged sufficiently, they will quite often produce the desired proposals. To make a consultant useful, the architect must be quite demanding until all possibilities have been brought to light, analyzed and evaluated.

Special Consultants

The architect has at his disposition a fairly extensive roster of specialists and consultants which can supplement his knowledge in the extensive field of building. When and how should they be employed to the greatest benefit? Architects, in general, have the habit of avoiding consultants whenever possible. This is quite understandable, since present fee schedules are not exactly generous. Clients, in effect, get what they pay for. If a consultant, for example, were engaged in the design of a kitchen, it would undoubtedly assure a better performance. But since the client is usually unwilling to make a special payment for a kitchen consultant, the architect has the right to decide who does what consulting work, which may even include his own staff though perhaps of lesser expertise.

Yet the commissioning of the best possible consultant is exactly what the effective architect should do, even though such special consultant fees may come out of his own pocket. He has the obligation to perform for his client in the best possible manner. Therefore, when knowledge and talent beyond that of the architect is called for, he should engage a specialist. Also, the better performance will give him an advantage over his competitors.

Typical specialists who should be engaged are the following:

a) Foundations and soils engineers. Even though the architect's intuition may be instrumental in the determination of the kind of foundation work, the scientific verification is essential.

b) Landscape architects. I should like to assure the reader that good landscape architects have a great deal to offer. Even if an architect is a brilliant masterplanner, the more detailed knowledge of flora and external environment is extensive enough to have produced experts.

c) City planner. It is almost purely theoretical to argue the value of the city planner, since an infinitesimal number of cities have actually been fully planned. The field seems to lack reality. Yet, what benefit would be derived by mankind if cities were planned by experts! City planning is a recognized art and science. Although an extension of architecture, it is a field of highly special character and knowledge. If and when it should fall under the jurisdiction of the architect to decide upon large-scale masterplanning, he should indeed engage the appropriate expert.

d) One of the most neglected areas is architectural acoustics. While it almost ranks in importance with heating, ventilating and plumbing, it is a field which most architects either ignore or treat with exceptional inexpertness. I would like to add that mechanical engineers have no better knowledge of the subject. I most strongly recommend that a bona fide acoustical consultant be engaged wherever the slightest necessity for a proper acoustic environment is indicated. Sound transmission and room acoustics are areas of physics, almost totally alien to most architects. They should be left to the acoustical engineer.

e) In several areas of specialized building equipment, where the architect has only a general knowledge, it is advisable to seek advice from manufacturers, even at the risk of producing a design heavily in their favor. Among these manufacturers are specialists in kitchen design, theater seating, stage rigging and lighting, intercommunications, sound and video systems. Furthermore, building material specialists in plastics, glass, metallurgies, cements, asphalts, rubber, and so on, are very useful. Some caution however is in order to avoid wholly closed specifications of designs.

f) Of considerable benefit to the effective architect's image are those who supplement his presentation material. They are renderers, model builders, and those learned in the graphic arts. The effective architect should always bear in mind that most clients do understand the picture, though not the technical plan. If the architect has no great rendering abilities, he will harm himself by showing his own handiwork rather than that of the proficient renderer.

chapter 8

The Strategies of a Bid Within the Budget

T HE BID OPENING is the architect's professional Judgment Day. The figures read "aloud in public" or covertly behind closed doors reveal nearly the entire range of his professional performance and ability.

All the virtues and vices, the strengths and weaknesses, are bared within a few minutes. To many architects the bid opening is a moment of nightmarish cruelty preceded by great tensions and, depending upon the outcome, followed by anything from triumphant elation to dismal gloom.

A bid high above one's official estimate ranks among the more embarrassing things. What architect can entirely shrug off the feeling of shame over his failure either to design within the budget or to estimate correctly?

On the other hand, what a grand, nay absolutely superb, feeling to find you can bid within the estimate! How victorious the architect, simply triumphant over materials, wages, matter or mind! A victory equal to winning a golf match, a regatta or ski race — where skill, endurance and daring are needed no more than on the long treacherous road from concept to bidding!

Although the architect may claim his artist's right to sanguine reaction, he may not claim effectiveness lest he awaken to some very sobering consequences about the bids. The bid too high can become very dangerous to his professional career. An architect who cannot "deliver," as one of my best clients once said, is soon out of the game. In extreme cases this means back to the drafting board (someone else's) or into a civil service job. I have seen both happen.

A bid over the budget is usually forgiven if it happens for the first time. If it happens now and then, it does not impair one's good reputation. But if it begins to happen with great frequency, present and potential clients are lost rapidly.

Conversely, a very real way to obtain a commission is by being below the budget. Because it happens so rarely, it is an outstanding achievement of great potential. I recall an institution which employed several architects. After much promotional work I finally got to do a job. My lowly status changed to a position of respected prominence when my little project was the only one in the past six years that came in below the budget. No amount of promotion could have done the trick so well as being able to "deliver."

Cost Control Starts with Program

The bid within the budget starts with the program. Here quantity and quality of the proposed construction must be fitted into the budget. It is perhaps the most difficult point at which to make an estimate since information available is most scanty. An advantageous method, therefore, is to reverse the cost of estimating a program: in the reversal the building is subdivided into elements, e.g., blocks of areas and spaces, and for each block a firm cost limit is set. Quantity and quality within each block are then adjusted. Fortunately, no one at this point has very firm concepts of anything; the estimate therefore is nothing more than a general monetary definition of the project.

The First Estimate

Many architects argue that once a budget has been established subsequent estimates (other than the periodic re-issuance of the official budget figure to satisfy the contract) are not necessary since the project cannot exceed the cost limit of this budget. To follow this highly theoretical line of thinking is one of the surer ways to have one's project exceed the available funds. The effective architect must clearly understand that the repeated estimates are a matter of very necessary self-control on one hand and a constant index for any alteration of the scope on the other.

At the beginning, the architect should realize, and may even take advantage of the fact, that estimates are not as binding as they will be later on. Therefore, the first estimate, which is based on fairly definitive schematics, should be as conservative as possible. The owner may growl at the high square foot cost but the message has been delivered.

One of the most common methods to make a reasonably valid estimate is to base cost on one or several square foot multipliers. The method has only general reliability since so very much depends on materials, structural framing, complexity of details, site; but most of all on the vertical dimension. Hence, a prerequisite for this method is the solidification of qualitative characteristics.

A further determinant is the fluctuation of construction costs. Most significant therefore may be the time factor, which in the last few years has seen increases of 10 to 20%

per year. These figures are of such magnitude that, if they are not taken into consideration, projects are abandoned with increasing frequency. An architect to whom abandonment has happened is not likely to forget.

Of course, the time factor is a most difficult one to pin down. But it is possible to keep a close watch on as many bids as possible and constantly compare notes with colleagues and contractors. An architect is very foolish to regard the high bid of one's colleague as a sign of inaptitude. It is certainly more prudent to regard it, first of all, as a cost indicator for that particular time.

There are some very common and often disastrous mistakes the architect can make at the first estimate. One is to disbelieve one's square foot figures because they did not fit the program. How often has it happened that a program required say 63,000 square feet with an available budget of 1.1 million (those were the days!), but the estimate shows 1.4 million! To disbelieve one's square foot figure of 22.20 and substitute with 17.50 is not only completely unrealistic but reveals great uncertainty in estimating. Once a square foot figure has been established, it should not be tampered with. The intention to reduce quality a bit, cheapen material here and there and use the lower figure to please the client is Utopian.

Another mistake made even more often is to base estimates on the lowest bid of previous jobs. Theoretically, this may be correct under the argument that there is always a low bid; yet incorrect it is, because bidding is not a rolling of dice where probability yields a certain distribution. Also as everyone knows who makes it a practice to analyze bids, there is usually a bunching of several close bids, known as good bidding. Then there are the out-of-the-ballparkers and once in a while someone is incredibly low. In 99 out of 100 cases, the extremely low bid is withdrawn or permitted to be withdrawn, since it is the result of someone's error. What remains is the solid center of which the arithmetic mean is the most reliable future cost indicator. Unfortunately, it is common practice to quote the low bid as the cost of the project. If all architects would quote the arithmetic mean of the 50% center bids, clients would be less often misled into huge programs on too small a budget.

A final word of caution. If an architect leaves his home ground to design a project for a locality unknown to him, he should bear in mind that construction costs vary tremendously with the geographical area, primarily because of availability of labor. I advise architects to investigate the area so that some comparisons can be made. Construction in a remote area, where no local labor is available, may be 100% higher than in a city only fifty miles away.

In summary, the conscientious, cautious and rather conservative first estimate, taking all known and determinable factors into account, is the number one stratagem for a bid within the budget.

To Restrain Owner from Adding

Undoubtedly a most frequent cause for the too high bid is the habit of owners to enlarge on the scope in continued small increments, until the budgetary balance has been upset. There are good reasons why it happens so often.

The client wants to obtain the best possible bargain. If there is a choice of several materials, he will, of course, want the more expensive one. When attempting to visualize a function in a room, the predominant result is the request for enlargement. The client employs a form of self-delusion often paired with greed when he enlarges the scope. The delusion is based on the primitive thought that the few little things he has added will never show up in the overall cost picture, similar to the delusion that eating between meals does not really add calories. Just as the scales disprove the latter theory, so does the bid opening the first.

I should warn my colleagues of one particularly annoying situation which is not uncommon. I am speaking of public or semi-public work where agencies or subcommittees are in charge of the various facets, such as planning or financing. The latter does, with understandable realism, set a firm figure. The planning group on the other hand will dictate a program not necessarily related to the budget, with the argument that they are responsible for adequate planning. Without straining my memory in the least, I can recall a fair number of buildings where the "owner" followed this approach.

In either case, the architect is in a most awkward position. Psychologically he fears that any denial of the client's wishes may endanger his good standing. Professionally, he has a certain pride and the ill-founded confidence that he can indeed pull the rabbit out of the hat — if need be, several times. He also is given to a certain carelessness: the estimate was an estimate, after all; nothing is so firm that a few more square feet would matter or that a material which costs forty cents more per square foot could not somehow be worked in. Because these additions come intermittently, they appear as far fewer than they really are. Therefore, the slight uncertainty about the validity of one's estimate, together with professional pride and fear of disappointing a client, has led many an architect to go along with the piecemeal increase in scope. I would say that the majority of bids over the budget are due to an unbalanced scope, a scope which was usually reasonable at the beginning.

One of the key stratagems for a bid within the budget is therefore that scope and budget always remain in proper relationship. If the owner increases the scope, immediate adjustment in the budget must follow. At this point the effective architect is faced with a tactical issue. Should he produce a new budget figure for every little change? My experience has taught me that a new total figure as such is necessary only periodically. However, the client must be informed that the change has occurred and will be reflected on the next estimate. Forbearance with a client would be very wrong. I know it is not easy to tell him that every time he makes a suggestion he has added to the cost. However, his tactics are hardly noble since he engages in a mild form of blackmail.

Therefore, the increase in cost must be stated sooner or later — the sooner the better. I recall an institution for which I designed a good number of buildings. Their method of adding was a variation of the two basic client techniques: their maintenance departments would issue specifications and design guides for the mechanical and electrical equipment. Most of the spelled-out requirements amounted to goldplating the project. In one building in the order of three million dollars, the new design guide increased the cost by $150,000! Most irritatingly, the department was, although quite subaltern, powerful enough to have its way. Yet no one in planning attributed any monetary significance to their specifications. Within days of receiving the new regulations, I informed planning of an estimated increase of $150,000. While my rapid countering was interpreted by some people in planning as a rash act of a typical architect under pressure, the issue did have legal value.

In summary, the best strategy is a firm stand on scope increases and great conscientiousness in maintaining records of additions, as well as the issuance of new estimates. The client has thus been informed at least. The responsibility has shifted to him.

The Final Estimate

Shortly before the bid opening, preferably within a few days, the owner should be presented with a final estimate, which already reflects any document changes through addenda.

While an intermediate estimate upon completion of the preliminary design has defined the cost rather well, only during working drawings and specifications do structural system, complexity of details, floor, wall and ceiling finishes, extent of mechanical systems, appointments and site work assume their final form. By then the client has also poured over plans long enough to ask for all kinds of changes and increases in scope.

The final estimate must take all these matters into consideration and should, therefore, be a full quantity takeoff. It is highly recommended that pricing only be done by an experienced estimator or, if this is not possible, that prices be obtained from contractors directly. I have at times used extensive, well prepared cost-estimating manuals. I can only say I have found such manuals highly unreliable. It is simply not possible to foretell future construction costs, which is what these manuals essentially attempt to do. Construction costs are very temporal, depending on many factors the manuals cannot take into consideration.

In the final estimate two points of caution should be observed in particular. In the first, the estimates of consulting engineers, such as mechanical, plumbing and electrical, should be mistrusted in principle and automatically increased by 20% before they are even entered into the summary sheets. The second point includes contractors' overhead taxes, job superintendency and profit. Contractors are naturally reluctant to divulge any of these figures. The architect can, however, with tact and reason obtain at least a safe range from some contractors with whom he is working. If no figures are available, I have found that a flat 20% added to the total estimate at the very end is advisable.

Invariably the final estimate exceeds all previous figures and often comes as a shock to owner and even architect, but it is a significantly less violent one than the sky-high bid.

Also at this point, cost reductions in planning can still be made and, if necessary, the bid date be postponed.

Guide Index for Estimates

Project Superintendency
Job-site Administration
Permits

Bonds
Insurances
Taxes
Job-site Facilities
Temporary Power
Demolition
Protection
Clearing
Grubbing
Excavating
Grading
Shoring
Concrete:
  Foundations
  Walls
  Columns
  Floors
  Sidewalks
  Curbs, Gutters
  Prestressed
  Precast
Reinforcing:
  Bars
  Mesh
  Cable
Structural Steel
Light Steel
Masonry:
  Brick
  Block
  Stone
Carpentry:
  Beams
  Arches
  Columns
  Joists
  Rafters
  Stud Walls
  Girders
  Sheathing
Roofing:
  Built-up
  Shingles
  Metal
  Tile

Lath & Plaster:
  Cement
  Gypsum
  Suspended
  Dry Wall
  Acoustic
Millwork:
  Doors
  Windows
  Cabinets
  Paneling
  Misc. Trim
Metal Doors
Roll-up Doors
Store Front Material
Glass
Decorative Stone, Marble
Ceramic Tile Work
Quarry Tile Work
Aluminum Windows
Resilient Floor Tile
Carpet
Wood Floors
Stone, Terrazzo
Hardware
Insulation
Acoustic Materials
Folding Partitions
Architectural Metal
Painting
Bath Accessories
Miscellaneous Specialties
Chutes
Metal Screens
Conveyors
Elevators
Turntables
Hoists
Fire Escapes
Fire Proofing
Railings
Theatrical Equipment
Special Decorative Finishes
Skylights
Toilet Partitions

Built-in and other Furniture
Drapes
Telephone Booths
Sound Systems   _____
    Subtotal

Mechanical)   25% to 35%
Plumbing   )   of subtotal
Electrical   )

Contractor's Overhead
  and Profit   (15%–25%)
Contingency   (3%–10%)
Time factor   _____

    Total Job Cost

Alternates

If indicated at this point, the realistic approach is the introduction of alternates. Alternates provide a somewhat flexible top to the cost which, in fact, makes them transitional to the negotiated contract.

Alternates have become, therefore, an essential tool because of our particular practice of stipulated sum bidding. Contractors have an instinctive and justified dislike for alternates. It decreases their single chance of being low because of the uncertainty as to which alternate the owner will eventually accept, and which not. Alternates vary, of course, with contractors since they depend on many things – like his relationship to subcontractors, suppliers, or his own abilities and personal inclinations.

It is, therefore, one of the important rules for the effective architect to choose alternates which are simple, clear and fully circumscribed; particularly useful are manufactured items, choices of quality or brand, or entire subcontracts. Disadvantageous are reductions of quantities, such as deleting entire buildings or portions of buildings. The theory behind this is to make alternates noncompetitive and of low imponderability, thus avoiding loss of the bidder's interest. As imponderability increases, complexity of strategy of bidding increases accordingly. The bidding contractor who can complete his bid no earlier than thirty minutes before opening time does not have the tranquility of mind to consider, let alone maneuver with, subtle strategies. The result is a safe and, of course, higher bid.

Whether an alternate is deductive or additive is of surprisingly little consequence. Architects often mislead themselves into strange paths of thinking. For example, it is frequently argued that the additive alternate is lower than the deductive one because the contractor in the first instance does not necessarily add profit and overhead, whereas in the second he does not necessarily deduct these items. The contractor's ability to bid is thus grossly underestimated. I have never in my entire professional life witnessed an instance where the contractor failed to recognize either adding or deducting profit and overhead relative to the alternate's designation.

The matter is entirely different when it comes to the owner. Generally, the American mind prefers the rock bottom base figure regardless of how cut down an item it represents, and secondly a choice of optional accessories. That very psychology which added only supposedly imperceptible amounts that would not change the cost, is now of advantage. Most owners will associate the base bid with the true cost of the building and attribute the additional cost of alternates more to their own spendthrift. The architect, therefore, appears in a better light if he has produced a low base bid. I should interject a word of caution though. If a base bid represents a project so cut down that its proper use is endangered, the results are, of course, very unsatisfactory. In the interest of everybody and as a matter of fairness, the architect should keep the client informed of the scope, in base bid and under alternates.

With this cautionary measure it is always better to employ additive alternates if there is a free choice.

Field Reputation and the High Bid

The architect's past behavior (and the resulting reputation) in the field may greatly influence the cost of his work. I will here describe the two most common errors in the field, errors which often cost the architect good standing, and the owner money.

The first error is running the field by the book. Running things by the book means an insistence or adherence to plans and specifications, not because of the end result but because that's the way the contract documents spell it out. This error is committed mostly by the younger and less experienced architects or by inexperienced field personnel. A colleague of mine has the reputation of being so unreasonable that bidders add a "factor" of 3% (the factor is locally named after him) to the bid. Another colleague of mine experienced, after a few years in business, growing revenge from the construction industry because of his haughty and inflexible behavior in the field. His bids were not infrequently 30% or more above the budget. I, myself, am not without guilt — in the first years of my practice I too insisted most readily on strict adherence to the written word. Fortunately, an older and more experienced architect tactfully pointed out to me the disadvantages of my rigid attitude before my reputation suffered greatly.

The effective architect must use common sense when he is confronted with a contractor's wish to deviate from plans and specifications. He listens to and evaluates new suggestions and employs reasonableness to arrive at a decision. Because he can legally enforce adherence, he should be doubly cautious not to impose his powers unnecessarily.

The second error concerns subcontractors. Not too long ago, the low bidder on one of my projects was a total stranger to me. Because we had never worked together, I asked this man why he bid my project to begin with and why he was low to boot. His cryptic comment was, "We had our ears pretty close to the ground." What he inferred was a sound grass roots (as we say nowadays) relationship with subcontractors and suppliers. Since subcontracts often amount to more than 80% of a project, rapport is of greatest importance.

Unreasonableness soon marks an architect in the industry. For example, if a column is poured two inches out of place, it would be simple to order it torn down and poured correctly. In most instances an error of this kind can be corrected other ways. The unreasonable thing is to insist on rebuilding. I recall one project where the tile setter reversed the ceramic tile colors in the men's and women's washrooms. The good man was willing to tear out $1200.00 worth of tile and replace it. After brief examination of the situation, I decided to leave things as they were. No one but the architect would ever notice the difference! Here unreasonableness would have corrected a minor error but left everyone with a bitter taste, to be reflected in future bids.

Timing

To time a bid the architect must take into consideration several relationships:

  a) General timing as related to the economy of the construction industry.
  b) As related to seasons — climatological influence or length of labor contracts.
  c) Bidding activity of other projects near or at the bid date itself.

The first relationship is the least consequential and also the one which can be influenced the least. If an industry is very busy, interest in additional work is low and prices are accordingly high. The fluctuations between boom and regression are relatively slow — usually a matter of years. It is, therefore, often impossible to wait for a better bidding climate. Cautious pre-bid estimates are the only safeguard against surprises emanating from relationship *a*.

Seasonal influences vary of course with latitude, but should be taken into account even in mild climates. An ill-timed bid in countries where frost and snow prevail would be one which prevents the contractor from closing in before winter starts.

Labor contracts are fairly predictable to the extent that expiration is known. After that date, wages always increase and the bid figures are affected accordingly. At times it is possible to arrange bid timing so that certain key trades can complete their work prior to the expiration date. Generally, however, I have found it to be the smaller risk to ignore labor contracts. It is nevertheless prudent to keep the client informed about the possibility of unpredictable cost increases due to new labor contracts.

Interference between several projects which are bid together or in rapid succession, two hours apart for example, can simply not be proven. I have attended endless strategy meetings in which all but the architect had their say with regard to timing, where every project near and far was taken into consideration, the work load of prospective bidders accounted for, and from this the most cunning sequence devised. What invariably happened was that those contractors who, according to scheme, should have bid declined to do so; that other bids did not turn out the way they were supposed to; that in general a whole new set of circumstances emerged which thwarted all grand scheming.

Another factor which enters occasionally is a favorite bidder's requesting postponement of the bid date to suit his private schedules. Such requests should be rejected summarily.

From countless experiences I can recommend that bid dates once set not be changed. Almost never is anything gained and usually the architect becomes known as a pushover if he yields to individual pressures. What is, however, important is the right amount of time to prepare bids. Again, neither too short nor too long is most beneficial. Practice seems to indicate that the bid period should be related logarithmically to the cost of the project. Illustration 8.1 shows empirically established values of this relationship.

The architect should also consider two minor stratagems which can influence the enthusiasm of the bidders. One is the penalty clause. I have found it best to have no penalty clause if no provable damage to the owner could be incurred. Furthermore, practice teaches that penalties are rarely paid, since owners will eventually accept most reasons for lateness.

The second is the permitted length of construction. Again, when the completion date is not a matter of great importance, it is far better to let the contractor decide upon the length of time it will take him to complete the work. One must not forget that it is in the contractor's best interest to do his work as rapidly as possible, since long drawn-out projects invariably cost him money.

The Good Bid

When the low bid is within the money, one usually celebrates and, upon recovery, prepares the construction contract. All this is relatively simple.

Bid Too High

When that happens, and it happens four out of five times, the architect will be quite busy for the next few weeks. Also the relationship with one's client becomes tenuous. It is almost inevitable that accusations are hurled around and that a search for the culprit is underway. I have often found that the ensuing thunderstorm is not without its merits since, as I mentioned previously, the owner is often a bit guilty himself. In a

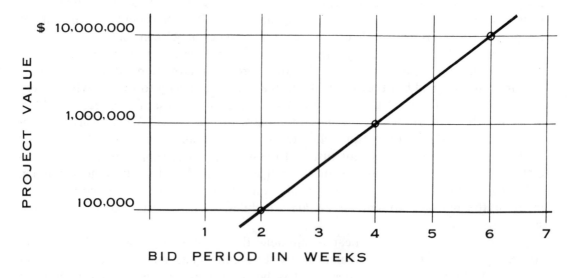

Fig. 8.1 Bid period relation to project cost.

controlled sort of free-for-all the architect at least has a chance to air his feelings too, and few owners emerge from the skirmish untainted.

Nevertheless, once the goat has been identified, it is the architect's burden to correct the situation. Most often the owner is then financially indebted to the architect up to completed contract documents. I have always considered it a matter of personal noblesse not to press for payment at this very moment but to restrain myself until the client has indeed an acceptable bid.

When the bids are over the budget, four avenues of approach are available:

a) Raising the funds to the new level.
b) Negotiating downwards; usually no more than 20% reduction can be achieved.
c) Re-bidding after appropriate changes to the contract documents have been made.
d) Abandonment.

Avenue *a* should only be suggested when the bids are in the ballpark; that is, no more than 10% over the budget. Surprisingly often the owner has additional funds in reserve. Avenue *b* is the most common and, therefore, is discussed in greater detail below. Re-bidding is only then indicated when changes of such magnitude can be made to plans and specifications that the new bids do promise a figure within the budget. No particular percentage can be attached except that a re-bid is usually indicated if the lowest bid exceeds the budget by 20% or more.

Avenue *d* is the least desirable. It is quite damaging to the architect's reputation and often his finances.

Negotiations

To reduce a bid figure to an acceptable level is not easy. Since it is foreign to the architect's entire thinking to alter construction, design and scope to a lower level and to bargain with the construction industry, exacting procedures should be employed to make it successful.

The architect must be aware of his position during negotiations. First, he is in the act of correcting what essentially is his error. Psychologically this puts him at a disadvantage. Secondly, he inevitably must accept someone else's advice in matters heretofore his sole prerogative. While his position was somewhat weak before, he now must humble himself and seek help and advice from "the other side." The architect whose pride prevents acceptance of this situation (and I know many) will not be able to negotiate successfully. As unpleasant as it may be, the effective architect does come to grips with the situation rather than jeopardize his reputation and possibly lose the job and the client as well.

Analysis of the Cost Breakdown

Before anything else can be done, the architect must analyze the cost breakdown of the low bid. If a well prepared estimate exists, the analysis is quite simple. The total cost should then be broken down into separate blocks, such as the various trades, subcontracts, manufactured items and built-ins. After separation into blocks, the areas of primary responsibility for the high bid will be revealed. Almost immediately the consulting engineers' blocks can be clarified and, if out of line, be given back to their respective authors for processing.

The majority of high bids display two broad patterns: either all items are proportionately higher than the estimate or only a few are completely out of line. The procedure therefore demands across-the-board reductions in the first instance, and isolated but radical changes in the second. The pattern must be recognized since the approach is not the same.

Cooperation with the Low Bidder

Although the architect's position is, as I mentioned above, not one of conspicuous grandness, the low bidder is far from being in the driver's seat; neither are his subs and materialmen. There is one thing the low bidder knows: if he cooperates in the reduction of costs, the project is his — if not, a re-bid is a virtual certainty. Subcontractors and suppliers are in similar positions. The architect will therefore find the low bidder quite cooperative, a situation which somewhat levels the otherwise biased negotiation atmosphere. Also, it is in everyone's best interest to conclude negotiations as rapidly as possible. The architect should therefore immediately set down a timetable for everyone, with a final deadline.

Technical Assistance

It is inevitable that, in the search for cost reductions, the advice of everyone should be sought. In particular, from the trades involved directly. The architect should, however, limit the range of alternative suggestions primarily to materials and simplification of details. Esthetics should be invaded last.

I have found it most advisable to conduct meetings with subcontractors whereby technical alternatives are discussed openly. Whether the architect will admit it or not, the broad experience and advice of the main subcontractors usually does lead to substantial cost reductions, without necessarily reducing quality a great deal. Once an alternative has been considered promising, the respective subcontractor must be asked to re-submit the new figure to the general contractor, together with complete descriptions of the alternative. Usually an adjusted test bid is put together when the majority of trades have re-submitted. If within range, negotiations can be brought to a conclusion.

Mechanical, plumbing and electrical costs are at times the sole cause for an excessive bid. If the analysis shows this, the respective engineers must follow procedures similar to those described above. Usually, however, a change of system will become necessary. If this is the case, in particular in mechanical equipment, great caution must be exercised to avoid the unbalancing of operation and maintenance costs. The client should be kept fully informed of all changes in the operational characteristics.

Re-Assemblage of Bid

When all trades, subcontractors and general contractor have committed themselves to new figures and alternatives, the revised bid must be reaffirmed and submitted to the owner. It is then a matter of necessity and fairness to explain to the owner in detail what changes are being proposed.

Adjustment of Contract Documents

Often in the rush of getting under construction after the successful negotiation, the architect disregards the most important facet: the proper amendment of the construction documents. If this is not done most thoroughly, the ensuing confusion and misinterpretations of what has been agreed upon can become quite serious. I have, therefore, found it to be most worthwhile to conclude negotiations in three successive steps: (a) reassembly of bid figure and client approval, (b) amendment of all applicable drawings, schedules and specifications, and (c) official re-issuance of amended contract documents and submission of a new firm bid by the contractor. In this manner the project is again accurately defined. Contracts can then be written and construction begun.

A Typical Case History

Some years ago I had a project for which the lowest bid exceeded the budget by nearly 20%. The client was willing to accept a negotiated figure if it did not exceed the budget by more than 7%, but stipulated that the floor area should not be reduced. The two conditions were so stringent that I doubted any success; nevertheless, the prospect of reworking the contract documents and re-bidding was even less inviting. I began with some simple but radical steps; I divided the scope into all major phases: concrete, masonry, plastering, air conditioning, plumbing and so on. Each phase was negotiated separately with the general contractor and his lowest sub. Against the general contractor's advice I did not permit re-bidding of subcontracts. Once everybody realized this and also that should we not reach the 13% reduction, the whole thing would be re-bid, I had established real team spirit. Furthermore, I set an early deadline so I could benefit from the immediate and current interest of all parties involved.

Only after setting down and checking the guidelines that every item must be reduced in cost by redesign, substitution, or both, did I accomplish the objective. At the end of one week, I returned to the client with a new figure showing a reduction of nearly 14%. The project was completed in the allotted time and has functioned well.

For the reader who would like to hear more about bidding, I will relate one of the favorite stories of my associate Donald Gadbery.

One of the bidders on a car agency he designed some years ago lived over a hundred miles from the place of bid opening. On the bid day, this man decided to drive by car and deliver his bid in person. The opening was at 2:00 P.M. In the morning, sundry things held him up and he left finally around 11:00 A.M. Halfway, his car broke down and frantic emergency repairs were made. Because of lateness he tried to hurry, only to have a minor collision as he entered the city. He talked the other party into letting him go to the bid opening, which they agreed to after he left his credentials. Within a few blocks of the bid place, he was finally caught for speeding. With a last grand effort, he persuaded the officer to let him go to the bid opening. The policeman agreed only if allowed to accompany him. The contractor finally arrived at the building at exactly 2:00 P.M.

As a matter of habit, his bid figure was not written into the bid form as yet. As he entered the building, a telephone call was waiting for him with a new figure from his office. This figure he did enter and, licking the envelope, entered the bid room at 2:02 P.M. Somewhat aghast faces greeted him and his unlikely escort. Two bids had already been opened. Even so, he humbly asked still to be let in, which was granted him after some grumbling by the other bidders. With the last bit of strength left in him, he collapsed into a chair under the incredulous eyes of the police officer.

At the very last — his bid was opened. He was second low.

chapter 9

Architect's Errors and
What to Do About Them

THE SYSTEM UNDER which architects work is not only unforgiving for errors but also paradoxical.

For all stipulated sum projects, plans and specifications may not (at least not theoretically) contain a single error. The system assumes perfection in the architect's performance. There simply is no fund to cover omissions, ambiguities, unworkable details and failures because of misjudgment and professional ignorance. And in all reasonableness there should be no such fund. Within the system therefore the architect is liable, again theoretically, and should consider all other parties involved free from accountability.

The paradox arises from the necessity to experiment with the new, while retaining a position of absolute technical safety. An architect cannot really risk any unorthodox or untried design, detail or material for which he is financially responsible should it fail to work. But if he does not engage in some experimentation or at least the courageous use of the new, his art will decline relative to those who are willing to accept the risk. He, therefore, can neither afford to gamble nor can he afford not to do so.

The ideal situation is to accept the risks of experimentation and win. Furthermore, a rather desirable position is one where one's plans and specifications are indeed without error or omission.

To reach either goal is, due to inevitable human imperfection, not quite possible. Nevertheless, a pretty fair approximation is practically attainable — a status where experimental risks can be reduced to insignificance and errors per se largely avoided.

The effective architect, therefore, must first know the causes of errors and then employ cautionary measures which will minimize their financial magnitude. In the following I will discuss the more common and troublesome errors and their causes, and then deal with preventive methods.

The Simple Mistakes

Only a few weeks ago a friend of mine (architect, of course) told me of a nasty little dimensional error that was made on the basement plan of one of his buildings. The building's nominal plan dimensions were 120' x 160'. Above the first floor slab, all exterior walls for several floors were 8-foot-wide precast units with 4-foot-wide double T's of matching floor assemblies. So far so good, except the outside basement wall dimensions shown were for some unexplainable reason 119'2" x 159'2". The walls were built that way, but the mismatch was not noticed until all precast for four floors had been delivered to the site. The error could not very well have been discovered in the shop drawings either since they were based on the upper floors and therefore in agreement with the upper floor plans. No one had compared basement plans with precast shop drawings. The job superintendent couldn't be held responsible either. The error was indisputably the architect's (my friend's). Well, from the first floor up, the building projected 4 inches on all sides over the outside walls. It took a fairly nice shelf angle, drilled and anchored into the wall, to provide the additional support for the precast walls. My architect friend lost $1680.00 for a small drafting error.

But dimensional errors are not the only ones. So very often one and the same item is detailed in two or more scales and in various combinations with other parts of the building. In the process of copying, enlarging and re-illustrating the thing, errors can so easily creep in. To construe an implication from several such details to the benefit of the architect is not only unfair but absurd. Or was it the intention to have this one door "trimmed" down to 4'7" because a beam was coming through right about where the door head was shown?

Quite annoying are contradictions between specifications and plans, in particular between two materials of substantially different cost. On the other hand, it is embarrassing when the "job super" calls you into the shack because he is a bit confused: he points to a loose end on the plans which contains the wonderfully simple notation "see spec," then turns to the appropriate spec section which says "shall be as indicated in plans."

Ambiguities

By definition, an ambiguity in the contract documents is a statement in lines or words which could have more than one meaning. Invariably, interpretation is then to the benefit of the interpreter. Ambiguities in either plans or specifications are rarely brought to light before the bid opening. "Discovery" occurs during construction. I have known contractors who in the preparation of their bids have become aware of ambiguities but waited until the tactically appropriate moment to spring these on the architect.

One of the particularly common danger areas in specifications is the quotation of manufacturers' or ASTM numbers, which are no longer in force. The reason for ambiguities in this field is the widespread habit of copying one's own or someone else's spec without actually checking the number of (and reading through) the quoted ASTM spec. It is in most instances better to cite one name brand with known qualities. The argument is often advanced that this practice causes manufacturer's representatives and architects unnecessary work in the approval process of equals. I disagree. Submittals for approvals of equals will always appear because the representative will take no chances. For example, to compare ASTM numbers on catalogs is far simpler at this point: one also has the opportunity to become acquainted with the product.

Another kind of ambiguity often quite costly, is the naming of equals which, when really compared, are not at all equal in either quality, function, or cost, such as roofing types and hardware lines. Again, it is better to let the equals emerge during the bidding than to have two irate manufacturers castigating the architect because the third man with the lesser product got the subcontract. If clients hear about such things, they have every right to have the architect render an account of what happened.

Drawings fare no better. Quite often some items were not firmly established in the preliminaries. Chances are then that notations of plans, sections, elevations and schedules, in particular with regard to materials, are inconsistent. The draftsman or team captain waivered over what to use and the final checking missed the inconsistent notations. To make such protective statements as "large scale drawings take precedence over small scale . . . spec over drawings ...," etc. is often too broad to be a foolproof weasel clause.

A Detail Will Not Work

Architects who have never built something with their own hands, who have never gotten a feel for the strength of materials or rigidity of static systems, are particularly prone to design details that will not work. Those who lack such practical experience are also the ones who over-design to the point of ridiculousness. I once came across a steel garden gate about which a client had some complaints — it was hard to swing and it scraped the floor. Looking the situation over, I found the gate alright, built of 1 1/2" square solid bars with alternating architected ladder-type grillwork. The gate was, due to its weight and completely unbraced design, deformed into a parallelogram. That's why it scraped. The reason why it was hard to move was its inertial weight of 1250 pounds. Fortunately, the grillwork permitted easy climb-over during periods of complete inoperability. By then I learned that the striker plate was already No. 3: the other two were sheared off from impact. I furthermore observed that the hinges were completely loose, ready to break out. I hate to admit that this incredible monstrosity came from the board of one of my better people. This is one example: I could fill pages with others. The point is that in errors of this kind we are not dealing with experimentation or calculated risks, but plain ignorance. Mistakes in this area are usually of a dimensional magnitude that could have been realized physically, if the designer had to build the respective detail with his own hands. It is perhaps the only "advantage of the disadvantage," as one of my nephews says, that these mistakes are not too costly to repair. One very important exception exists, however: if a $40.00 mistake exists in a component which occurs 2000 times in a building, run for your life. If an architect designs a repetitive building component, the only correct approach is the construction of a prototype, at his own expense, to assure proper operation.

Functional Errors

These are the ones which owners delight in pointing out to everyone. The door that would not open more than 45° into the bathroom because it hit the lavatory. The straight sight line from all sorts of vantage points right into the toilets, usually the toilet bowl itself. The "opaque" glass that does not screen out but acts like a movie screen. The two consecutive doors made to hit each other with gusto. The thousand and one cases of misplacement of windows, so that anyone not looking constantly at the floor is subjected to blinding brightness. The walls with good sound transmission. The toilet door with the big air-intake grille. The light opposite the mirror. The apartment windows and doors vis-a-vis each other, so conducive to brotherly love. The beautifully curved archway with blood stains everywhere except the very center. The grand terrace steps for exalted living: too short for two steps, too long for one, (hint: make them traverse diagonally). The noisy machine room air intake in the delightfully landscaped inner court. The interesting intersection of a stairlanding with a corridor the other way (suggest: have them blow their horn like the Alpine busses in blind curves). The inswinging window that tears the drapes a little bit more every time. The window swinging out into the passageway, so easy on the human frame. A counter too low (try drafting on a coffee table). The light fixture way up there. How do you wash those windows? With long poles! No, I mean now that they are up there. When it rains one can clearly see where the gutter and downspouts should have been. The lonesome column in the entrance way. The dividing partition that fits the building module, nothing else. The light switch on the hinge side: better yet, on the opposite wall. The unexpected change of level in the middle of a corridor does a fair job to sprain ankles. Door knob neatly breaking adjacent glass panel when swung back. Specify wall-mounted items where there isn't a wall. The 17 walled room to fill in between way-out planned rooms. Mirror in toilet so placed as to reveal otherwise well hidden bowl. Fountain in front of entrance: delightful spray machine in wind. Loading dock connecting the store room through 300-foot tunnel, 4 feet wide. No garbage chutes in high-rise apartments.

  Perhaps my readers would like to enlarge this checklist for future use.

Major Errors

A major error is one which (a) must be remedied and (b) is of some financial magnitude. For example a high-rise building has been standing for almost ten years. Its exterior is clad with glazed terra-cotta tile cemented to the wall. One morning a tile $2' \times 2' \times 1''$ has left its place high up and lies broken in myriad pieces on the sidewalk. Ten days later, two more tiles fall down. Within the following four weeks, a total of 24 are shattered on the sidewalk. Still there are many thousands in place, each a potential killer. Soon the area is barricaded since several tiles now come down daily. There is no question left in anyone's mine that all will come down. Something must be done immediately. An impartial investigation shows that the architect has specified the wrong mortar mix. Estimated cost of adequate removal and substitution; $75,000.

If this happens to a firm of modest financial strength and one without errors and omissions insurance, and if the applicable law has no statute of limitations, an error of this kind can well spell the end. One of the great dangers from which the architect must protect himself is to underestimate the importance of certain details. The importance increases in proportion with the size of the project — so do all risks.

Major Malfunctions

They are usually due to the design errors of mechanical or electrical equipment. For example, a building may be underpowered due to insufficient transformers, feeders, switch gear and so on. Unsuitable equipment may have been specified or outright errors in computations been made. Quite generally electrical equipment is particularly susceptible to the repetitive error since the majority of switches, fixtures, outlets, panels and so on occur in great numbers on identical pieces. One error may therefore mean one thousand errors.

Heating, ventilating and air conditioning is no safer. In fact, errors are nearly always most costly still. Misjudgment, miscalculation, the wrong choice of equipment, and wrong controls with such things as wrong zoning, are among the most common. If everything else works, there is often the matter of noise and vibration. Plumbing has some specific features other equipment has not: liquids flowing through pipes and valves, hydrodynamic forces, expansion and contraction due to changes of temperature, and chemical reactions, are all too often not sufficiently taken into account.

The point of significance with the mechanical, electrical and plumbing malfunctions due to errors is the involvement of the consulting engineer. Whatever the arrangement with him may be, the architect must clarify the matter of financial responsibility. I have made it a habit to spell out next to the fee, that the consultant must assume full financial responsibility for his errors and omissions. If it appears necessary, proof of insurance has to be rendered.

The Structural Failure

Nightmare of all errors is the structural failure, collapse or condemnation because of unsafe condition. Not only are these errors the most costly of all to correct, they almost always involve litigation, since negligence is often involved. In some instances, structural failures result in injuries or even fatalities. Structural failure is something the architect must avoid at all cost, even if corrections must be made with monies out of pocket (or through insurance). The architect of the building is nevertheless a marked man. There are no excuses for structural failures. The most daring buildings are still standing, like the C.N.I.T. shell, towers, bridges, Gothic cathedrals, space frames, hypars and so on.

The failure which is not a collapse as yet but renders the structure unsafe is the one for which the consulting engineer must also have insurance, by proof of financial responsibility or insurance proper. The failure reveals itself usually at the beginning of construction and can then be repaired.

Not always is the structural consultant wholly responsible; quite often the contractor and sometimes the architect, by default, must assume partial blame. The architect may commit an error of omission by not supervising construction so adherence to plans and specifications at least is assured. He may furthermore be morally responsible if he has made undue demands upon his structural engineer. Ultimate design is one thing, but to endanger the structural frame by excessive material reductions should never be undertaken, even if no governing code exists.

Avoidance Before the Fall

Architecture is difficult enough. The last thing the architect needs is to be plagued with errors, mistakes, omissions and failures. Because errors do occur, the effective architect must strive to keep occurrences to a minimum and avoid bigger mistakes altogether.

There is no magic formula for the avoidance of errors. However, certain systematic approaches to every project are basic preventatives. There are a few principal rules which I have found to be the best safeguard.

Rule No. 1 is always to prepare very complete and exhaustive preliminaries. No significant feature should be left out or remain undetermined. The structural system with all major dimensions must be completed so that no surprises emerge. Likewise, mechanical and electrical systems must be designed and generally sized. Finishes should be fully established.

Rule No. 2 is to maintain at all times a clean, orderly structural frame. Form may follow function but in the case of the structural frame, functions must often compromise. It is furthermore useful to separate the structural frame from architectural drawings. In this matter, the frame will show itself most clearly and complications as well as omissions become glaringly evident.

Rule No. 3 is a function check-out. Walk through your plans, peer right and left, open doors, imagine you are in the structure, look for windows, ceilings, structural features, look at walls (wall elevations are very useful).

Rule No. 4 concerns specifications. Although the Zeitgeist produces more and longer "computerized" specifications, the drawing with as much information as possible is the best safeguard against errors and omissions. Also a clear and irrevocable demarcation must exist between what goes into the spec and what on drawings. Should the plan only say hardwood and the spec define it as walnut? We have a tendency to streamline by producing a terribly complicated system. Again, simplicity is the key.

Rule No. 5: No plans should leave the office without having been subjected to a thorough check. Nothing quite measures up to that.

Rule No. 6 states that the architect should make use of the knowledge of the many minor specialists whose knowledge of a particular component or material far exceeds his own. He simply cannot know the whole range of everything.

Through observance of these rules, most potential difficulties have been avoided at the outset. Of course, nothing can be perfect and errors are certain to escape even the most ardent plan checker. These errors are then carried into the field and must be dealt with during supervision.

chapter 10

Successful Construction Supervision

UNDER MOST FEE structures, supervision constitutes 20 to 25% of the total services. Even though the work is extensive and complicated, much of it does lend itself to systemization, and thus has the potential of good profits. To assure that these profits are made, all possible areas of trouble which may interfere must be avoided or minimized.

The technical part of supervision, that is, to check, test, devise alternate solutions and administer funds, is taken for granted. It is the essence of the supervision work and usually is not the point of difficulty.

Herein discussed are the areas of trouble and methods to avoid and minimize them. Furthermore, guides and procedure systems are presented in three crucial areas: Field decisions, shop drawings and change order records. In conclusion, methods of learning in the field are outlined.

The Field Decision

It would be incredibly naive to think there is one single building that was built according to plans and specifications. In most structures hundreds of details deviate from either the drawn line or the written instruction. There are many reasons why this is absolutely inevitable.

To point to the major ones, there are first of all the inevitable errors on both sides. Plans have omissions and mistakes and the contractor makes mistakes. Next, most contractors soon discover labor and material saving methods over those they had worked out during the bidding. It is a matter of course that resulting alternatives will involve deviations from the contract documents. The architect's demand of rigid adherence is often foolish and rarely serves any useful purpose. In fact, obnoxious behavior will be remembered on future projects and the bids go up accordingly.

Then there is no plan or detail, so perfect, that it could not be improved upon or done differently. Changes are often an absolute necessity because conditions are so complicated that alterations are unavoidable if the structure is to be buildable.

Furthermore, the fluid stream of commerce and industry causes constant changes in materials, products and delivery schedules. This results in unexpected unavailabilities of materials and components, necessitating the acceptance of alternate products. Then again, changes in performability of subcontractors and suppliers, transportation, deliveries, labor market and issues referred to (strangely) as acts of God, are all causes of deviations from the planned path. These causes in particular call for a continued adaptation to new situations.

In the vast area of private work, contractor and architect usually have the freedom to adjust to new conditions and seek out the most advantageous alternatives. That is the prime reason why private work, generally speaking, is less expensive than public work with its highly inflexible practices.

Successful supervision depends on field decision. Its limitations are defined in the general conditions: the adaptation to a new situation under the premises that neither will additional cost be incurred nor will the intent, meaning and scope of the contract documents be altered.

Yet it is unavoidable that the field order will cause changes of construction cost. Technically speaking, all additions or deductions are subject to change orders: practically, however, official change orders would not be to anyone's benefit, but become the source of much paper work and possible friction. Last but not least, the impression on the client, who knows little or nothing about the subject and its complexity, would be quite disturbing. To him it would soon appear like an unsolvable mess of errors and incompetencies on all sides.

To avoid change orders for every field decision, supervision has adopted as part of its very meaningful terminology the word "horsetrading" and the phrase of "give-and-take on both sides." The purpose, of course, is that credits and debits are being equated as they occur. Most often the issues involved do not alter anything significantly enough to warrant a special record. If they do, the record will simply become part of the as-built drawings.

The successful management of give-and-take, equating errors and favors, alternative solutions and materials, is the true art of supervision. It requires intelligence, diplomacy and, of course, a most thorough technical background. Yet, with all these prerequisites, the actual mechanics of equating remain fairly difficult.

The architect must realize that everything that ran according to previous plans will remain unrecorded. What did not go as planned, therefore, is the substance made up of field decisions. Therefore, the record of the field decisions is the record of supervision itself.

We have worked out in our office a system for the processing of field decisions. This system does three things: it records the subject matter, establishes a value and aids in the balancing of debits and credits.

In practice it works as follows. Let us assume that construction had just begun and the contractor discovered the omission of several thousand pounds of steel in a particular stem wall, to which steel must be added. The field order record would then show the quantity, where it was missing and the cost to add the steel. This cost amount is then shown in the column of credits to the contractor. At this point, we might possibly make the decision whether or not the owner should be informed, for the purpose of having the question of payment cleared, or whether we should pay for the steel ourselves.

As a next entry in this example, we would show that the contractor had requested the use of old plywood to form certain walls, rather than the new plywood spelled out in the specification. The walls in question are either plastered, tiled or furred out. The surface appearance, therefore, is quite unimportant and the use of old plywood no detriment. The field decision, therefore, is to grant the contractor's request. At this point, we establish a reasonable value of the savings by negotiation with the contractor and enter it as a credit on the architect's side. As we go further along, the contractor may have placed a series of sleeves in the wrong location, which would change the routing of some steam pipes, the lowering of a ceiling and sundry other little adjustments. To break through the concrete and place the sleeves correctly would involve cutting through tensioning cables. A field decision is therefore made to adapt everything else to the new situation. Since the solution was beneficial to the contractor, again a reasonable value is worked out and placed on the architect's credit side. Next, our drawings show a window sill detail displaying some very serious deficiencies in the manner in which it sheds water and protects the wall below. The solution is the widening of the sill and increase in downward slope, and a different method of caulking. The field decision, therefore, is to use the altered design. Again, a commensurate credit is entered on the contractor's side. Possibly at this point, a balance is calculated. It really makes little difference to whose debit or credit the balance comes out. As the work progresses, debits and credits usually begin to equate closer and closer.

At the end of the project we have a perfect record of: first of all the field decision, then the cause, and finally the responsibility. We, as architects, have also gained an impressive index of our errors, which by feed-back are used to reduce errors in future projects.

Analyzing the contractor, a great deal can be deducted from his record as well. A good picture of his tendency towards, and ingenuity for, alternative solutions emerges. Also, the quality of his operation is rather well revealed. This is very useful to know for any project where the architect might be instrumental in the selection of a contractor.

The Change Order

The change order should only be resorted to for actual changes in the scope of the work. In this respect, the change order is then primarily linked to the client and his instructions. As such, the process is fairly cut and dried and need not be discussed here any further.

I should like to add one point of significance, however. Once the project is completed, it is often very important to know who requested a change, for what purposes and with what justification. Change orders should, therefore, always be accompanied by thorough explanations as to who ordered them, why and what purpose the changes should serve. Great unpleasantness can be avoided later on when no one would quite remember why these decisions were made. When things don't work out, the architect is the first one blamed — in particular, when the individual who instigated the change is no longer in the picture.

Punching Out

To make punch-outs as efficient as possible, the architect first of all should bear in mind that he is not working for the contractor.

The architect who punches out too soon is, in fact, working for the contractor. Even though the documents require the latter to produce the completed project, which would involve the check out of all work and systems before the architect is called in, it is far easier for him to let the architect do the work. The effective method to avoid getting involved too early is to give the contractor who insists upon the punch list a little sample of what is coming. For example, the architect may take a small area which is obviously not in very good shape, and write one devil-of-a-tough punch list. When extrapolated into the whole building, it would be so extensive that the contractor might just as well take bids on it. When this sample is handed to the contractor, he should at that time be told with all authority that the work is incomplete; and on the basis of the sample all further funds must be withheld to safeguard the owner's interest. That usually will get him moving in the right direction. To simply tell him, after a brief visual inspection, that he is not ready, will accomplish little because no direct proof has been rendered to support the statement of incompletion.

Once the project is ready, the actual punch out is very important indeed. Like all processes of checking, it is far from simple, and unless somebody with a great deal of experience or personal adeptness is involved, the process is either lengthy or inaccurate.

In the interest of quality as well as efficiency, we had some years ago developed a checklist which in most instances left very little to memory or personal ability. The checklist follows the concept of systematic comparison and testing, and treats any internal space as a room with basic boundary configurations.

Figure 10.1 is a reproduction of the punch out form which confines itself to the substance, leaving out all verbiage.

Shop Drawings

It wasn't so very long ago that shop drawings constituted the better part of the working drawings. Architects prepared general plan layouts, sections and elevations, together with the basic structural frame. Most details were inferred and drawings prepared by the respective trades, many never to be seen outside the shop. Because of the general decline of craftsmanship, shop drawings today are little more than copies of the architect's working drawings.

In most instances, therefore, the architect must go through the wasteful procedure of

---

Punch Checklist

Step 1:   Check against plans to assure everything is complete and exists.
Step 2:   Check against finish schedules.
Step 3:   Check condition for any defects.
Step 4:   Check color.

Dictate punch item: First   — location or room number (once only, before punch list).
                       Second   — on what component and where.
                       Third   — condition or defect.
                       Fourth   — correction procedure.

General: Check for foreign substances on all surfaces.

Specific:

 1. Doors: fit, operation, paint top and bottom.
 2. Windows: fit, operation, seal, glass type.
 3. Floor covering: (tile, base) even joints (carpet), fit, joints, tightness.
 4. Plaster and drywall: surface, cracks, gouges, junctures at doors, windows.
 5. Paint and finish: coverage, surface, runs, sags, streaks.
 6. Wall covering: even, tight joints, adherence, (tap ceramic tile).
 7. Acoustical ceilings: even joints, texture, alignment, edges.
 8. Draperies: operation, track secure, fullness, straight seams.
 9. Millwork: operation (doors and drawers), workmanship, anchorage.
10. Ornamental work: details, workmanship.
11. Plumbing: operation, pipes secure, escutcheons.
12. Electrical: cover plate, fixture alignment.
13. Equipment: operation, model number, make.

Fig. 10.1

---

checking whether his working drawings were copied accurately. While most owner-architect agreements spell out the checking of shop drawings, it is unreasonable to interpret this to mean that any shop drawing coming from the contractor must be checked down to the last dimension. As a partial answer, many architects have elaborate stamps absolving themselves of almost all responsibility with the exception of some nebulous agreement as to "general design only." I have never considered that to be the solution of the problem.

Furthermore, to check work in the field the architect's working drawings are used for comparison. At that point one wonders why the architect was bothered with shop drawings at all. The present system is time-consuming, wasteful and imperfect.

The effective architect should, therefore, adopt a clear procedure. Shop drawings can be divided into two groups and processed accordingly.

In the first group are those which are a necessary technical definition, submitted by the manufacturer or craft involved. Shop drawings for such items require checking to the best ability of the architect. It is, of course, essential that the architect have had good knowledge of the item he specified and also diagrammatically inferred it in his drawings. What he must do, however, is reject any responsibility as to the function of the item. That indeed is the responsibility of the supplier. For example, elevators can be checked to see if they fit into a structure and what operational pattern they are programmed to, but whether they will work is outside the architect's realm and has nothing whatsoever to do with the shop drawings.

The second group is the pure copies of the architect's working drawings. They should be summarily disregarded.

I have over the years in my practice included the following instructions in the Special Conditions of the Specifications:

> "Where called out to be required, shop drawings shall be submitted in ( ) copies. The architect will check these for conformity to and suitability for the project. Dimensional correctness, operational functioning and interaction with other components are the contractor's responsibility. Whenever the contractor wishes to propose alternatives to any detail, manufactured or shop-built items, he may submit descriptive shop drawings for the architect's consideration. Any shop drawing which is a copy of the architect's working drawings will not be checked and returned to the contractor."

Incoming shop drawings are instantly separated and then treated according to this paragraph. This has raised efficiency by a considerable margin since the multi-sheet, multi-copy bulk which required initial checking and then a copying through of check marks, is thus avoided.

Consulting engineers, of course, may take advantage of these instructions as well. I have found it, however, preferable to leave it to their judgment to treat shop drawings in their own manner.

Rapid Processing and Recording

The architect must, if for no other reason than to protect himself, gear his organization to process all matters related to supervision as rapidly as possible. Furthermore, it is essential that virtually everything be recorded, even if it gets tedious. It happens quite frequently (whether justified or not) that a delay in the completion of construction is claimed because of tardy processing by the architect. In particular, when penalty clauses exist, very nasty situations can arise for the architect. He, therefore, must process rapidly and keep full records.

The two most important status records are those concerning shop drawings and change orders. A practical record which immediately displays the whereabouts and status of any shop drawings and submittal is displayed in Figure 10.2, and a similar record for the status of Change Orders in Figure 10.3. Both forms are employed in my office and have saved a great deal of time, primarily because they leave nothing to memory and require only periodic checks. In particular, the status as related to consultant's participation is under the full control of the architect.

Rapid processing, of course, must also be exercised in all matters concerning pay

Shop Drawing Status

from   to

Project: _____   Period: _____

Legend: GC = Gen. Contractor   Status: A = Approved
         SC = Subcontractor   AN = Approved as Noted
         SE = Struct. Eng.   R = Resubmit
         ME = Mech. Eng.   D = Disapproved
         EL = Elect. Eng.   CN = Copy of Arch. Dwgs.,
         PL = Plumb. Eng.   not checked

Title or Subject and Sheet Nos.	Date Received by Architect	Submitted by	No. of Copies	Architectural	Sent to	Date Sent	Date Received Back	Status	Final Distr. No. of Copies				Remarks
									Gen. Constr.	Engineer	Architect	Owner	

Fig. 10.2

requests. It is truly amazing what amount of goodwill can be created for the architect if pay requests are checked out on the very day they arrive and the certificate is issued immediately. Therefore the certificate of payment should be issued as soon as possible.

Change of Subcontractor

Whenever a subcontractor's list is required, be it by rules of public work or as a condition of the contract, the contractor is firmly bound to his subs as he lists them in his bid. Yet it happens on nearly every project that a change of subcontractor is requested by the general. Whatever the reasons may be, the architect should be the sole judge whether or not a change is justified. All reasons for the subcontractor's inability to perform are reasonable cause to permit change.

More difficult is the question of changing subcontractors to get a better figure or get

Change Order Status

from   to

Project: _____   Period: _____

Original Contract Sum: _____

Completion Date: _____

Legend: O = Owner   SE = Struct. Eng.
         A = Architect   ME = Mech. Eng.
         GC = Gen. Contr.   EL = Elect. Eng.
                               PL = Plumb. Eng.

C.O. No.	Date Issued	Subject	Amount (+) (−)	New Contr. Sum	Responsible	Paid by	Time Extens. Granted	Remarks

Fig. 10.3

involved in "bid peddling." While it would seem that this is a despicable practice, my experience has been that there are instances where "bid peddling" is in order. The classic case is a post-bid negotiation to reduce the figure of a particular bid. If the subcontractor refuses to cooperate, because he thinks he is protected by the sub-list, the architect should permit (if not directly suggest) negotiation with the second low and from there on down. The justification of this action is a matter of fairness all around. If the sub-list is there to protect the subcontractor against bid peddling, he should then be obliged to enter into negotiations. Of course, there is the frequent practice of subcontractors protecting each other and forcing the architect and general contractor to accept their dictates. But even under those circumstances, a certain amount of pressure can be brought upon him by threatening with re-bid. No group is so closely knit that there are no deserters — something the subcontractor knows very well.

Certificate for Payment

It is a general practice that the contractor claim more work completed than really is the case. His motives are that a 10% retainage exists anyway and that by the time he usually receives payment he has far exceeded any excessive claim.

While these extenuating circumstances exist, the architect who softheartedly signs an inflated certificate is taking a considerable and most unnecessary risk. Formidable complications could arise if a contractor defaults and the project was not bonded. If quantities as claimed are found incorrect, the architect must reject the claims and request resubmission. Some contractors have the idea that the amount is something that should be bargained over. In this case, the architect should never let himself be drawn into the position of arguing the correctness of his quantity back check.

It is one of the essentials that the architect be at all times sufficiently familiar with his project and have a good knowledge of the amount of work done. Furthermore, towards the end of the month he should be particularly cognizant of the degree of progress, preferably so much so that he himself has a schedule of completion that can be checked against the contractor's.

Subcontractors and Lien Waivers

According to Hoyle, the general pays his subs before he receives his payment from the owner. At the end, he makes final payment, receives the sub's lien waivers and then claims final payment from the owner. Clear and simple.

But practice is quite often different. The sub gets paid only after the general receives his money. At the end, the subs' only hope to get paid is to produce a lien waiver prior to the final payment. In many cases, the final 10% retainage represents subcontractors' money only; the general has taken his profit out earlier. This explains why so many generals are indifferent to the cleanup of final punch items. The general contractor's behavior on the other hand is somewhat understandable too; his share in the whole job is often no more than 25%. Why should he advance 75% to subcontractors? The cause for all this is, of course, that our contract forms are overdue for adaptation to prevalent practice.

What position should the architect take? He cannot but accept the contractor's signature that all bills are paid; he must accept the subcontractors' lien waivers as proof that they have been satisfied, even if he suspects they have not. After all, a subcontractor could theoretically refuse to produce a lien waiver.

If the situation is very critical, the architect might do well to inform the owner. It is, however, the owner's responsibility to take action. At this point it is often wise to involve an attorney.

Supervision as a Policing Action

This is usually what the client thinks supervision is all about. As the experienced architect knows, the policing part is the smallest of the whole area of supervision. Nevertheless, there are contractors who constantly seem to be tempted to cut corners and often are brazen enough to do so quite openly and unashamedly. This type of contractor could cause the architect a great deal of annoyance. It is therefore wise to employ strategies that will prevent that type of behavior from the very start.

As a basis for prevention, I have found most effective laying the law down at the start. To begin with, if there are no good reasons for a deviation from plans and specs, no deviations should be permitted. Furthermore, if the slightest bit of cheating is suspected, a check out of everything should be intensified to such a point that the contractor soon realizes the futility of his attempts.

On one building which I had designed the roof consisted of Single-Tees. We had no particular reason to doubt the proper manufacture and reinforcing of the tees. However, upon arrival at the project the tees exhibited about the worst workmanship I had ever seen in precast work. Cambers within 80 feet varied as much as 3 inches and flanges deviated up and down by similar figures. One of my inspectors, therefore, made a most careful examination of all visible components, in particular the flange weld plates. Upon tapping these weld plates, he soon discovered some that could be dislodged. Further tapping broke the plates free altogether. Figure 10.4 shows the weld plate with a 1″ long reinforcing bar as compared to the 3′ anchor which was specified. Needless to say, all precast tees were rejected. Had we permitted their installation, or not discovered the absence of anchors, the structure could with little live load imposed have collapsed.

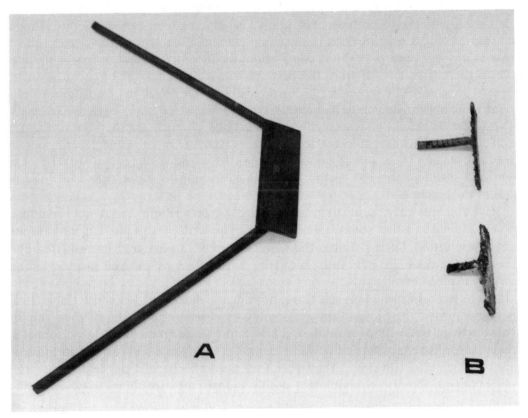

Fig. 10.4 The anchor plates labeled A were specified; those labeled B were discovered during inspection.

That kind of policing is absolutely essential. On the other hand as a power play, it serves little useful purpose.

The Field: A Place to Learn

The architect who does not utilize the field to the utmost as a place of concentrated learning is both foolish and arrogant. Nowhere is the opportunity for feed-back more profound, nowhere can so much benefit be obtained, as in practical comparison between plan and product. Architects cannot claim that it is impossible to learn in the field.

To make field learning most effective, the architect should employ a system. He must decide: (a) who should go in the field to learn; (b) what should be observed and studied; (c) how much time should be spent to learn.

Generally speaking, everyone who has worked on a project should see the results of his theoretical planning. To be more efficient though, a bit of grouping is useful.

The designer should study every facet, but will gain most toward the end of the project when final form and surface has emerged. He should make the most thorough study of the structural frame once it is completed. In particular clarity, or as may be the case, complexity should be studied since there is a relation between these characteristics and cost. In this respect, it is also most worthwhile to visit projects other than one's own, projects which have been known as very costly or very economic. The relationship to cost is least obvious in the completed building, when little else but finishes leads to any conclusion at all. At completion, the designer should pay particular attention to the key issue: is it truly the best servant of the function? I know it is difficult for any designer to be critical of his own creation — we are all in love with our designs — but some objectivity can be learned.

Next, details should be re-evaluated, perhaps not so much for the sake of the detail itself as for its fittingness in the total picture. Another broad subject is finishes, surfaces and color. These should be looked upon from the viewpoint of: (a) usefulness, wear and maintenance; (b) beauty — color relationship to material and intrinsic purpose of the building.

I have found it very useful to actually write a short critique about my buildings, as though I am discussing someone else's work. The written critique demands far more acute observation, since it forces the writer to think through and to evaluate impressions. Having done so, it is truly surprising what effect by delayed memory alone is carried into the next design.

If there were draftsmen on the team, or whoever determined constructional details, they should visit the project during assembly to observe the results of their thinking. Usually, there is no more than the scantiest feed-back from the field personnel and what there is is rarely instructive. Most construction details must be left to those who produced working drawings. They therefore need the benefit of field observations.

In summary, the effective architect should prepare a list of things to be seen and by whom. The field inspector must then inform the production people of the construction progress to permit actual visits at the crucial moments.

The benefits derived from the well-balanced field study program are better designs, uses of materials and cleaner construction details, resulting in spectacular reduction of cost.

Post-Construction Inspections

It is truly amazing what benefits arise for the architect who practices well organized post-construction inspections of his buildings. These inspections must be concentrated on the following:

a) Structural behavior; in particular, deflections, differential settlements, cracking, thermal movements;
b) Durability of finishes, where exposed to wear and in untouched areas;
c) Functioning of air conditioning, plumbing, electrical equipment;
d) Functioning of other equipment — elevators, folding doors, conveyors, etc.;
e) Usefulness as related to design, acceptance by owner.

The inspections should be spaced to follow the natural behavior of the building and its use pattern: once every two months for the first half year, then before the end of the first year (also to prepare the warranty punch lists), and then preferably once a year for the next three years.

The inspections do three very valuable things: first, they give a most thorough insight into behavior of one's construction; secondly, they show how the building is used and accepted; and thirdly, they provide for natural, continued contact with the client. In the latter respect, they also make a very favorable impression upon him; they prove to him that he deals with an architect who is indeed highly qualified and reliable.

The Client on the Job

By its very nature, this subject belongs in the next chapter. But a ground rule of pure behavior must be mentioned here. The rule states that the client, in his own best interest, maintains his contact with the field only through the architect. He must be told that contractors, subs or suppliers often tend to bypass the architect in order to obtain something the architect would not permit. This leads invariably to a lowering of quality and, apart from that, to argument and confusion.

To prevent that kind of problem from arising, the client should be informed, at the start of construction, of the organizational pattern. If necessary, he can be bluntly warned of the potential trouble if this pattern is not strictly maintained.

The Owner's Friend on the Job

There is a deep, psychological desire in the mind of the client for an impartial judge of everybody's performance. Therefore, if he perchance has a friend who claims real (but usually has pseudo) knowledge of the field, potential trouble is afoot.

To show off their knowledge, these doubtful characters will pick some inconsequential detail and explain how poorly the thing has been executed and inspected.

For this type of person, the architect has considerable defenses at his disposal. First, he should immediately ask the client to have his friend state the matter in writing. That is precisely what the pseudo superintendent doesn't want — to put his ignorance on record. Ninety percent will stop right there. Of those which are left, it should be requested that they recommend the proper correction or improvement and be invited to assume full financial responsibility. Beyond, it is best simply to ignore them.

Some years ago, I had a call one Sunday afternoon from one of my clients who had been out on a job with a friend of his who claimed expert knowledge of pipe welding. This man had made an inspection of some connections in the heating system and found things obviously not to his liking. My client was quite excited over it and suspected insufficient supervision (something most clients seem to suspect very frequently). The pseudo inspector was then put on the phone and told me that not even in his apprentice years would he have "come up with a job like them kinda welds on them joints." I immediately suggested that he give my client a written report of what he saw and, in addition, told him I would look into it. The first thing I did on Monday morning was to inquire in my own office about the situation. I had learned to my great satisfaction that the day before a pressure test had been conducted, that the welds were inspected and the whole system functioned flawlessly. I immediately sat down and wrote a letter to my client, maintaining however a diplomatic tone so that no one would be upset. The success was remarkable. My client's confidence in my field inspection, in fact in my entire behavior as architect, was fully regained and my reputation higher than ever. The pseudo inspector walked away relatively unscathed, but never again opened his mouth. The contractor, an exceptionally conscientious man, grinned from ear to ear.

chapter 11

Disputes and How
to Solve Them

To HAVE A project run its course without disputes between the various parties involved is of great importance to the architect. Disputes are, like wars, almost a complete waste and, in addition, seldom is anyone completely right or wrong. In business, disputes cost money for which there is no return and from which investment there is never a profit. The only possible justification is a fight to prevent an otherwise greater loss: to dispute with hope and intention to minimize such a loss. Disputes, even if settled, leave in their wake some permanent scars. The disputing parties are not likely voluntarily to engage in cooperative efforts again and, if perchance the stream of events pairs them again, much suspicion will drain away otherwise useful energies.

Quite clearly, disputes are best avoided; second best is to squelch them immediately; and, if inevitable, they should be approached with as much goodwill and earnest desire for settlement as possible.

I am by no means inferring that disputes, their cause and reconciliation are simple. One must recognize the causes of misunderstanding and distinguish between such things as the unintended error or the inflicted wrong, and lastly the difference of moral levels on which people in business operate.

In the field of architecture and construction, there are certain typical areas of dispute between any one of the three involved parties – owner, architect and contractor.

These disputes have definite breeding grounds and, as is well known, the vast majority do occur during construction.

During this period the architect is in quite an awkward position. On one hand he is the judge and interpreter of the performance of the contract between owner and contractor. In this role he must see to it that both live up to their obligations. Yet he receives compensation from the owner only, who of course expects to have his interests represented first. As a further complication, the architect is interpreter of the meaning of the drawings and specifications and thereby sets himself up as judge over his own performance, in opposition to the contractor.

The currently prevalent owner-architect agreement is largely responsible for this sequence of absurdities. The instrument is responsible for having provided by its highly artificial (and even hypocritical) meaning a rather fertile soil in which the seed of disputes is already sown. The duality of the architect's position thus created should, of course, be removed by altering the cause, i. e., changing the agreement rather than battling the effects. However, as the instrument only reflects current practice, the individual architect can do little.

This chapter discusses the more typical disputes, their causes, how to approach prevention and achieve solutions.

Owner and Architect

The first differences in the owner/architect relationship occur, if at all, when the owner rejects the first design and demands a second and possibly a third alternative. The architect has every right to refuse the preparation of alternatives. First, it was the owner's responsibility to use due care and foresight in the selection of his architect — he had ample opportunity to investigate the kind of work the architect would do for him, and secondly, unless the contract spells out alternative design, the architect simply is not required to follow such whimsical demands. Yet many clients seem to have the idea that the architect must prepare several designs so that they have something to choose from. The result is a dispute that easily leads to the dissolution of the contract. Usually the architect's only recourse to obtain payment for what he has done is litigation.

Like noise, which is best squelched at its source, this particular area of disputes can be avoided if there is a full and clear understanding before the architect proceeds with the first design. Some very early schematics may be produced as a test. In most instances though, the owner can't visualize anything until he sees either a model, renderings or fairly descriptive plans. And by then it is too late.

The area of greatest complaint by most owners is supervision. There are, first of all, differences of opinion over what constitutes adequate supervision. Of this, I have spoken in previous chapters. The differences, however, turn into disputes either when the project begins to suffer through inattention of the architect, that is, when the owner does not receive the value for which he pays, or when, on the other hand, the owner becomes delinquent in his payments for the architect's services. Also, the architect may have caused a delay in completion which, if of material detriment to the owner, is just cause for dispute.

Owners do exhibit strange forms of behavior at times. When he plans to build, he seeks the counsel of the contractor and often arrives at an arrangement that supposedly protects him from the ruthless exploitation of the parasitic architect and his exorbitant fees. But if he commissions the architect, he demands his protection against a cheating contractor!

Therefore, whether the project has suffered or the client only believes it has must remain a moot question; nevertheless, the preferred situation is that of a good relationship and happiness all around. Should the above dispute arise, the architect may take the following steps:

a) He makes an honest effort to listen to his client's complaints;
b) He politely requests from him actual instances of where and how the project has suffered;
c) He explains in depth why the project has not suffered;
d) He reminds him that he cannot guarantee the performance of the contractor;
e) He shows him the positive side – the many checks and controls that are built into the contract;
f) He makes a most thorough joint inspection with the owner in which all of his questions are answered.

More difficult are the "in cahoots" situations, when the owner conspires with the contractor. The situation is all too common and usually below the surface so as to make things fairly difficult. The typical situation in private work is where the architect is considered the necessary evil, or fifth wheel on the cart (a situation frequent in package deals), or in public work when contractors, due to their political influence, can wield power to benefit their interest. If the architect, in particular in the latter situation, refuses to be "reasonable" or to "cooperate," even "play along," things usually become quite unpleasant. Two results are most common: first, the owner will see to it that the architect's image is appropriately tainted, in particular that other owners hear about it, and secondly, there will, of course, be no future work. The architect is being hit where it hurts the most

In this situation the architect's defenses are unfortunately quite weak unless he is prepared to fight the holy war.

His first choice is, of course, to give in, to let the contractor have his way. But giving in is relatively ineffectual if it takes place after disputes are well along. It then means to the other parties that they have won, and they have tested and found failing the strength of the architect's defenses. If an architect decides to be the diplomatic politician who is a friend of everybody, he should show his true colors at the very beginning. At least, he will have an easy life. I know many architects who have chosen this path.

His second choice is to state all consequences with regard to structural instabilities, non-durable materials or what else the case might be. The statement should be in writing, detailed and sent to all other parties involved. To clinch the matter, the statements should be accompanied by a direct "I now await your orders" letter to the client. In personal confrontations the architect should not argue at all but repeat what he has written and then stand by for the owner's instructions. This, at least, places the owner in the position of having to commit the crime. As a further choice, in particular when structural stability is involved, he must either withdraw his seal or fight the holy war with press and public as his allies. To have even the remotest hope to survive that form of dispute, he should have substantial financial resources.

Architect and Contractor

Usually one of the two parties is more at fault than the other. Let me start with the erring contractor (we architects always do). The contractor who errs by design or habit may have an entire book full of tricks through which to gain his end. Of all the difficulties a contractor can produce, the two most damaging are insinuating to the owner that the architect is not supervising the job properly, and passively resisting the architect's instructions to abide by plans and specs. The contractor has much to gain if this two-pronged fork is applied properly. First, by criticizing the architect for not doing what he, the contractor, secretly does not want done, namely policing him, he often wins the complete confidence of the owner. Once he has that, he feels quite safe in ignoring the architect who "so obviously falls down" on his inspections. To give his position yet greater credence, simultaneously he attacks the architect with a barrage of change order requests, all for extra money to overcome mistakes and omissions in plans and specifications. Of course, all this is done with a great deal of fanfare so the owner hears every detail.

This kind of dispute usually starts if the contractor intends to get away with something and the architect is in his way. The "something" most often amounts to the entire performance: if it could be expressed quantatively, an across-the-board quality cut of "x" percent.

The foundation for an effective defense by the architect is to perform his duties correctly to a fault. He should ignore the contractor's noisy defamation; in that manner he can use his energies for more effective counteraction than continuously proving his innocence. Next, he must refuse to issue the certificates for payment when probable harm has been done. In this instance, it is very useful to make accurate calculations of how much money might be involved in corrections and offer these amounts for reductions in the requests for payment. Furthermore, it is absolutely essential that all actions and communications be recorded and such records kept in flawless order. In matters of communications, the architect is wise to maintain a strict matter-of-fact tone. This kind of contractor will seize upon the most minute cause as a justification to abandon all bounds of business decency.

By maintaining an impeccable position himself, the architect can at least hold his own in the continued disputes with this kind of contractor. Eventually, the contractor will by his very nature make other enemies until he is known for what he is. Patience on the part of the architect is simply necessary.

Between architect and contractor there may, of course, exist the reverse situation, where the architect makes life miserable for the guileless contractor. Avoidance of such disputes is simple if the architect admits he is wrong. Most codes of ethics of the architectural profession do in fact single out as a breach of ethics an architect's coercing a contractor to make good mistakes in plans and specifications. Because the architect has the final power to sign the certificate for payment, and because he is documented as the interpreter and judge of the contractor's performance and the spirit and intent of the plans, the slightest misuse of power results in disputes. True, it is always possible that the contractor interprets an ambiguity in his favor, but because the architect has reserved the right of final judgment for himself, it is he who is first of all obligated to interpret in favor of the contractor.

Once the contractor has had occasion to experience the architect's fairness, he is likely to accept his judgment even if unfavorable.

Owner and Contractor

The owner's disputes with the contractor are, although frequent and broad, rarely a matter of direct confrontations. The disputes are almost always carried on through the architect. Only if he as the emissary has become ineffectual, does the dispute become a direct one. Since the architect cannot guarantee the contractor's performance, he could treat any dispute between owner and contractor with considerable indifference, in particular if he has done everything required of him during the project and towards the settlement of the dispute.

Indifference is not the answer; the architect must always remember that responsibility in this area applies to him in particular: he did set himself up as the judge of the performance of both parties — now let him judge indeed and see to it that justice is dealt everywhere.

The causes for owner-contractor disputes are many. I will here enumerate the most frequent ones.

On the contractor's credit side of the ledger, the most frequent cause for dispute is the delay in or unjustified withholding of progress and final payments. No one is more culpable of this than governmental agencies. Extreme irritation is even more justified in such cases: the government has the money and only because of ill habits, indifference, bureaucracy and a desire to exercise power must others wait for their just compensation. Private owners often delay payment as well, roughly in inverse ratio to their affluence.

What can the architect do? First he must realize that he will have to admonish the client, admonish the very man who pays him, that he must live up to the terms of the contract. That takes a bit of courage! However, the client knows only too well that he is wrong and that there should be no necessity for admonition from the architect. And because the client knows that, the architect's action is usually quite effective.

If this step does not seem to be worth the risk of offending such an important party, the next best step is some advice to the contractor concerning his rights to shut down the job and to file liens. If the contractor on the strength of that advice only as much as threatens the owner, the latter is likely to correct his omissions.

Another habit of owners is amateur interpretation of contract documents. I have seen owners (and I really wondered by what authority) interpret contract documents to their sole benefit, reading specifications as they pleased and applying anything at all to whatever suited them best. In most instances, this kind of owner will call the architect and with a naïve form of hypocrisy suggest the "correct" interpretation of the contract documents, and finally instruct the architect to inform the contractor to that effect.

As unpleasant as it may be, the architect has absolutely no choice but to tell the client where he is wrong. If the latter has any decency, he will eventually see the issue as it really is. Otherwise, the courage and the honesty of the architect to insist upon fairness will in the long run be to his benefit. In the short haul, however, considerable annoyance can be in store for the architect. That is unfortunate but cannot be helped. As I mentioned before, it is a matter of behavior on a fairly low moral stratum.

And now, let's talk about the contractor as cause of annoyance and disputes. Perhaps the greatest single area of dispute with certain contractors is that they have little intention of following plans and specifications, even after they have repeatedly deviated and been reprimanded for negligence and digressions. This type of contractor intends to get his way by using such tactics as indifference, rudeness and playing stupid. With these attributes (incidentally one of the tip-offs of this type is his poor English sprinkled with obscenities), he intends to wear down the owner as his partner in the contract documents. It is most unfortunate that the architect is the one who gets hurt first because he stands between contractor and owner. To this contractor time schedules are nonexistent; he often creates much dust and noise, and otherwise harasses everyone with his boorish manners. Most frequently, the immediate originator is the job superintendent. Regardless though, he does speak and act for the contractor who is lastly the one responsible.

The situation is not a pretty one for the architect, but in most instances, controllable. The practical counter-measures which the architect as judge of performance can evoke are:

a) to give this contractor adequate warning, documented in a manner to provide evidence for possible litigation;

b) to prepare counter-claims if properties have been damaged, and to make the respective deductions in the very next payment certificates. The contractor can do little but make good and accept deductions; if he ceases to work, he places himself in a far worse position.

c) In the case of nonadherence to plans, specs and field orders, he must receive written notice that if corrections are not made before further work makes them impossible, a stop order will be issued. A typical case is a rough concrete floor which is not leveled before resilient tile is put down. The significant point is, however, that a stop order indeed be issued and enforced.

These disputes are legally between owner and contractor. It is very important that the architect assure himself of cooperation by the owner prior to any action. It does happen not infrequently that owners get cold feet when actual enforcement must take place. Equally often this kind of contractor seeks the sympathy of the owner in order to avert the architect's justified measures.

Another and very extensive area is the clean-up of final punch items and corrections to be made under warranty. Unethical contractors know that by using sufficient passive resistance they can get away with leaving a project unfinished in certain details, and

usually do not risk litigatio[...]
ready to admit that I know[...]
proponent of the enforcemen[...]
the construction cost to the end [...]

In conclusion, the reader may be [...]
tive matter only, where neither archi[...]
scathed. Architectural practice and con[...]
with disputes and antagonism. Otherwise, [...]

I would like to leave my colleagues with th[...] project without difficulties
is as rare as a jewel; let us enjoy those few.

chapter 12

The Necessity of Professional Publicity

PUBLICITY IS NOT only necessary for the success of any architectural office, it is also very beneficial for the entire profession. Admitted or not, the architectural profession does not command as much respect as it should from either the public or those connected more directly with it.

The public will care very little about architects until it has learned about architecture. Therefore, anything which brings before the public good architecture is of direct interest to all architects.

This chapter discusses the paradox of publicity in architecture and methods of conducting publicity on an individual basis. It also proposes a new form of architectural exhibition.

It compares the methods of publicizing the constituent segments of the architect's make-up: the artist, engineer and the businessman. Finally, how to put across the story of a project is discussed in detail.

Where We Stand

Amazingly little has changed for the architect in the last 150 years. Anyone who has read Talbot Hamlin's near tragic account of Benjamin Henry Latrobe must admit that the architect's problems have not diminished and his image has barely improved.

Today, there are few technical areas about which the public is less informed than architecture. Most people know more about heart transplantation or atomic physics than by what principles of structure and space the buildings that immediately surround them function. That the public knows next to nothing about the architect is painfully evident.

The architect can only blame himself. Rather than going out and educating the public, architects have been so busy with the process of policing one another that they have almost missed the point of their purpose in society. By creating closely controlled groups, architects hoped to win the same respect from the public physicians and lawyers have but this plan has, frankly, failed. The architectural profession is full of individualists and deserters. Therefore, architects as a group could not have been anything but ineffectual in the education of the public. To be sure, The American Institute of Architects has initiated several programs in this area. Quantitatively, however, these are feeble efforts. The systematic education of the public about architects and architecture on a nationwide basis, intensively pursued, does not exist. Bearing in mind the nature of the architect's make-up, such concerted efforts are not likely ever to come about.

Publicity of the Individual

Because architects as a group have proven to this day that they are relatively incapable of delivering their message, the individual architect should not only be permitted and encouraged to, but must, conduct educational publicity about himself.

Until quite recently, any publicity or advertising was done at the risk of being severely censured. In Canada, it could cost one's license.

As a natural subterfuge, quite a few architects employ a public relations agent. Others have elaborate brochures printed. Most will bend over backwards when reporters call for a story.

But in the total picture, only a few engage in publicity for their firm: the majority remain silent because of uncertainty how to advertise, the possible consequences from the professional community, and the cost.

Let me make several things clear. The very lubricant of business in these United States is publicity. It is the vehicle by which one's existence and product are made known to others. Our entire society operates on the basic premise that he who wants to sell must appeal to him who is expected to buy.

The architect seems to think himself exempt from this pattern. He wants things in reverse: he does no more than set his name out on the doorstep, and those who plan to build must find him. Now isn't that absurd? By what elevated status over his fellowmen does the architect reserve that kind of lofty behavior for himself?

My dear colleague, you will readily answer: lawyers and doctors do not advertise and they are professionals like us! The very point is that architects are not professionals of this kind. Architects are a combination of artist, businessman and engineer.

And how do these three propagate their name and skills in our society?

The artist is the original "free sketcher." Almost everything is first created, then exhibited and, depending on quality and name, sold. I place art first for the reason that design ability, artistic talent, is the only component which the public will fairly readily recognize as belonging intrinsically to the architect. Depending upon the architect's artistic ability, the public is interested in his creations.

The substantial organization of The American Institute of Architects is virtually unknown to the public. But a single man, a single architect who challenged his society with his ideas and artistic talent, is known by almost every educated American; Frank Lloyd Wright has done more for architecture than the thousands of committees which sat and talked. Even the U.S. Post Office decided to disseminate his name.

As long as architects claim any talent in art, the ways of other fine artists should serve as a better example than a confused, disputed and askew system that does not admit the artist to architecture because of its supposed need for professionalism.

The Architect Exhibits as Artist

In my high school years in Lucerne, Switzerland, the great artists of that country like Victor Surbek and Paul Zehnder, had frequent showings of their paintings. It belonged to the cultural habitus that these showings were discussed in private and public, that almost passionate likes and dislikes developed — not of artists so much as of various paintings of the artist.

In a manner of speaking, architects nowadays do a similar thing with their awards programs. But the showings are primarily of grotesquely manipulated photographs of buildings. They become the inverse of what they should be — an educational stimulant for the public. The displays show the image of the building not the building itself. The technology of photography with its filters, variable focal lenses, cunning printed techniques and graphic assembly, shows this image with unnatural skies, unnatural lighting conditions, totally unrealistic contrasts, distorted or altered angles, artistic large-grain tele-shots and so on.

These methods neither display the building to the public nor do they represent even a comparable image. As a media, it shows two-dimensionally something that has three dimensions. It is apparently taken for granted that the viewer can accurately imagine himself standing in front of or inside the real building and, of course, also perceive the psychological feeling the building emanates. To make the situation more absurd, the exhibiting architects are not in the least interested in the public's reaction. Their concern rests with the ruling of the jury or awards committee.

The Effective Architectural Exhibition

I, therefore, propose that the public display of buildings should be vastly modified. Once that has been done, it should be used as a frequent medium in every suitable community to bring before the public at least that which it can grasp: the three dimensional creation as seen from without.

First, I propose that no architecture should be exhibited unless it is in the form of a representative scale model. I furthermore suggest that within each showing all models be of the same scale, of similar technique and landscaping. The display room must have as lighting a high intensity source to simulate sunlight and sun angles.

Secondly, the public's participation must be invited. To let the public walk by, as is common with photographs on display boards, is not enough. The public must be enticed to render an opinion. This can be done by having a polling box at each model and asking the visitor to deposit a "like it" or "don't like it" slip. It should be rather interesting to count the likes or dislikes at the end of a good day.

Furthermore, a most definite effort should be made not to have a competition among exhibiting architects. Therefore, any such thing as a jury composed of experts, who will pass learned judgment and, consequently, influence public opinion, should be avoided. It is far more important to learn of the public's preferences. The practical method is a polling of the public as to their overall first, second and perhaps third choice.

Finally, I would propose numbering the exhibits rather than using the architect's name. In this manner the public will not discuss architects but architecture: opinions stated will not be of architects but of visible and tangible structures.

The system does not exclude the possibility that the names of the architects will eventually be connected with the most liked structures. But that isn't really the point.

The Businessman's Publicity

The architect as businessman should at least be aware of the businessman's way of publicity. I do by no means propose that the architect should employ the prevalent boastful, deceptive and misleading forms of advertising. Yet there are many forms that tastefully project a firm's existence and products. The kind I am talking about are, for example, the monthly advertisements of Kodak as they have appeared for years in *The Scientific American* – pleasant, informative and with a touch of humor. Although the day has not arrived quite yet when architects are "allowed" to advertise (it will happen!), architects can and should advertise as a group. The tenor should be educational – what architecture is, what the architect does, what his services include and how he serves his fellowmen. While a beginning of it does exist here and there, infinitely greater effort must be put into it, and for far longer periods, before the effects will manifest themselves.

And the Engineers

Engineers on the other hand have no inhibitions about advertisement. In fact, their ads are rather well placed, as the sample, Fig. 12.1, from one of the leading construction journals, demonstrates.

At least the engineering firms reach out directly to their best customers, the contractors. The ads are factual: next to name and address, they state range of services offered – but again the architect is not ready to adopt even the ways of that third of his professional Gestalt.

Fig. 12.1 Engineers' Advertisements

The Story about the Building

Most news media are interested in bringing to the public a story about buildings, in particular, when much money is involved or the structure has social significance. There are other reasons too, but they all are more on the sensational level, such as a building really far-out or one that has collapsed. It is important for the architect to bear in mind that the news media are not doing this out of love and charity for him, but because their livelihood depends on a good story.

If the architect wishes to benefit also (as he most certainly should), it is he who can make the story good and interesting. To accomplish this, he must himself prepare a write-up: descriptive, non-technical and with emphasis on those points which concern the human element. Secondly, he should make suitable graphics available — diagrammatic plans, clear and easy to read, and good photographs. Most reporters take from supplied data what they please and reassemble it in their fashion, often unrecognizable, misquoted and possibly slanted. But without the well prepared data, the story would be chaotic, trimmed only to appeal to a desensitized public appetite for sensation. The sensation if not achieved by some remarkable feature of the building is often conjured out of a negative triviality (for which reporters have the noses of bloodhounds).

There is seldom a well designed structure that does not have one or several remarkable features which are of interest to other people. Not too long ago my firm designed facilities for a turntable manufacturer. The business of making turntables is quite specialized, but could really be performed in almost any kind of manufacturing space. A seemingly dull assignment such as this can produce one or two unusual ideas and, when publicized properly, give the otherwise untrained reader a momentary glimpse at something worth knowing and of interest to him. The building in question was eventually written up in a well-known construction magazine.

I had prepared three pages of general notes about the basic design problems and structural frame. Together with these, I submitted several diagrams, which were faithfully reproduced. A comparison below shows that my notes and the story as it appeared were in remarkable agreement.

Significant quotes from:

Architect's Write-up	*Story As It Appeared in Magazine*
I suppose it can be said almost with certainty that Mr. Carr has constructed the only manufacturing plant in history for the sole purpose of building turntables. When he outlined his requirements to me, I could truthfully say that there was no precedent from which I might draw prior knowledge and experience.	The owner is also a resourceful man. His intuition told him that his production could be facilitated with a round structure. ...
The requirements for a turntable manufacturing plant would seem simple enough. Mr. Carr outlined a central assembly area, to permit as large a turntable as possible to be preassembled prior to shipping. ... The deciding step in the solution of the problem was to build a circular assembly hall. It was obvious that in contrast to other manufacturing functions, Mr. Carr did not need square feet as much as he needed diameter; thus the circular shape permitted nearly 100% use of the actual square foot area. In the final design, turntables of 112 feet in diameter can be preassembled.	As the owner states it, "The architect came to the irrefutable conclusion that, given a modest unit area cost limit, and since the production space required was for making turntables in excess of 100 ft. in diameter, the main portion of the building, for economy, had to be round." In the architect's words, "In contrast with other manufacturing functions, the owner did not need square feet as much as he needed diameter. Thus, the circular shape permitted nearly 100 percent use of the actual square foot area."
The most difficult problem created by the circular shape was that of the crane. Quite obviously, all conventional systems were unworkable. For this reason, I proposed a crane which consisted of a	The architect noted that, "The most difficult problem created by the circular shape was that of the crane. Obviously, all conventional systems were unworkable. For this reason, I proposed a crane

rotating beam. This beam is centered at a thrust bearing and suspended from a circular track on both ends. Two hoists will travel along its 112-foot length. This crane not only solved the problem, it also presents some rather new and intriguing operational patterns due to its ability to describe circles as well as radial lines.

which consisted of a rotating beam. This beam is centered at a thrust bearing and suspended from a circular track on both ends. Two hoists will travel along its 112-ft. length. It presents new operational patterns due to its ability to describe circles as well as radial lines."

The Free Lance Story

Another practical method is the classic article, treatise or paper on an interesting subject in architecture. Such subjects may be anything from an account of a study trip, to a current issue of a much discussed proposal for a public structure. If an architect engages in this form of publicity, he serves not only himself but the entire profession, since he places before the readership purely cultural matter. The point, however, that most architects overlook is that their stories are written in a professional tone, above the heads of most laymen. Therefore, these stories find their way mostly into professional journals and not into publications which are read by the people at large. Therefore, the free lance writer must observe first of all that the subject about which he writes has indeed public interest, that the tenor is on the laymen's level (which means that most technological matter is avoided) and, of course, that the article is written well.

The Office Brochure

Depending solely upon the inclination of the individual architect, his office brochure may be large or small, display quantity of building, or only a few explicit pictures, or it may be mostly data of personnel and completed structures, or have a bit of everything, or, he may not have one at all. There is no simple best pattern.

The brochure will, more than anything else, match his mode of working. If he is accustomed to highest standards in his practice, he will demand the same of his brochure. If he is a production man, his brochure usually is crammed full. In both instances, it is a reflection of the performance of his office.

Because many architects are pretty fair graphic artists, they often layout and assemble the brochure themselves. I consider this a distinctly good habit, much to be encouraged. But the architect who designs his own brochure must keep foremost in his mind the following:

Brochures should:

a) Be interesting.
b) Be beautifully done, dignified.
c) Describe the firm's philosophy.
d) Introduce principal(s), and not too much staff (that is usually boring).

e) Show good pictures, not fakes, even if there are only a few. (Plans with the pictures are usually of interest.)
f) Show site plans.
g) List completed structures, with construction year and cost. If there are not enough, the last could be left out.
h) Introduce some educational thoughts about architecture, and the services of the architect.

In this regard, my office brochure has always stressed the last point. The important point is that the language, although technically correct, remain in layman's terms.

Figures 12.2 through 12.7 are the six initial pages from my office brochure. As the reader can see, layout and technique are extremely simple — six typewritten pages and several simple pen sketches. Whenever I present this brochure, these pages secure the immediate interest of the prospective client, since the context is of concern to him as layman, about to make history with an edifice in his own sphere.

N O   M A N

can be indifferent to architecture. It provides for us the artificial environment in which we pursue our many activities. We all partake in the creation of
buildings, be it in planning and constructing, or in the approval of the edifice.

A structure, accepted as practical and pleasing, is a cultural accomplishment of
the entire society. The society's needs dictated size, location, quality and
beauty. Those who have decided upon these determinants have thus acted as architects; they have projected a need into the material reality of buildings.

Since mankind existed, architecture was its most obvious product. It is
therefore fascinating to look back and ask ....

Fig. 12.2

WHERE DID IT ALL START ?

The first real buildings known to us were the temples in Asia Minor, Egypt and the Mediterranean.   3,000 years ago, these magnificent structures set the stage for all architecture.

The "Greek Temple" was a rectangle of columns, surrounding a solidly walled chamber.   A gabled roof, resting on beams over the columns covered the building.   Simple and beautiful.   It was an architecture of stone, subordinated to the material.   The proportions and ornamentation of the components adorned the buildings and gave them their classic rules of esthetics.

More engineers than architects, the Romans developed the arch and its three-dimensional expansion, the vault.   Buildings with large, column-less halls could now be built.

Fig. 12.3

But more important, the span between two supports could now be bridged by small stones and brick. For the first time, the limitations of gravity were pushed back by man's ingenuity.   The arch was used in houses, public buildings, aquaducts, bridges and gates.   Its existence dominated the world of building for about a thousand years, culminating in the highly advanced and beautiful romanesque churches.

Shortly after the year 1100, French masters began to point the romanesque arch.   Next, they removed all walls and supported their building on intricate systems of shafts and crossed, pointed arches.   In further defiance of gravity, the flying buttresses were invented.   As the most incredible, most orderly and beautiful of all architectural styles, the Gothic came into existence.   Within less than 100 years, it reached its culminating perfection in the great French cathedrals.

Fig. 12.4

But the heights of the gothic spirit were not endured very long: about the middle of the last millenium, mankind grasped for a less complex and more playful style. Elements from the past, the greek classic and romanesque were merged into new forms. In the medieval City State of Florence, renaissance emerged. Within a short period it had virtually spread throughout the civilized world. The great Baroque buildings of central Europe are the end product.

Then came a time of boredom. Man reached for anything of the past. The period of the re-births came, Roman, Greek, Gothic, even Egyptian were unearthed. It was a time of decadence for architecture.

Fig. 12.5

OUR AGE

The great advances of technology in the last century provided new materials: steel and concrete. Together with mathematical discoveries, these materials provided the foundation of modern architecture. New forms became possible. With exuberance did man grasp for the new building elements. The great French engineer, Eiffel, attained heretofore unknown heights in steel. Nervi of Italy became the father of concrete architecture. Artists of design and mastery of material, like Le Corbusier and Mies van der Rohe set new lines of direction. The skyscraper shaped the modern cities.

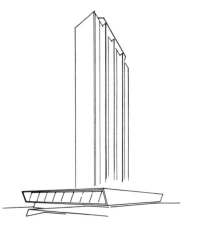

Technology advanced farther, giving architecture high tensile steels and the stressing of reinforcements. Bridges with spans approaching a mile, roofs arching over many hundred feet could be built.

Fig. 12.6

TOMORROW

Our frontiers of building technology, where present and future meet, concern themselves with the mathematical sculptures of shell architecture, with the advent of plastics and ferro cement.

The ever-increasing research of use and function, lower costs, higher quality, sophisticated interior appointments, metals, plastics, resilient flooring, new discoveries in lighting and climate control, acoustic conditioning of an environment, all have made our buildings more efficient, safe and comfortable.

Architecture does not stand still.   As a continued expression of technology and culture it must be placed at man's service, for his physical well-being and his spiritual ascend.

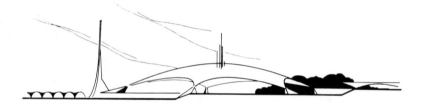

Fig. 12.7

chapter 13

*The Architect's Position in
the World of Building*

THE ARCHITECT'S PUBLIC image is quite important. It determines the value of his work and the respect his knowledge, responsibility and leadership obtain. The practical resultants are the height of fee scales and ease or difficulty of his professional career.

An image of high esteem therefore must be the constant concern of the effective architect. To serve this cause he should know what his image was and is now, why it has declined and what can be done to bring it back and maintain its prestige.

What the individual architect does characterizes the professional community and conversely the character of the community labels the individual. The two are completely intertwined.

The architect can do much to elevate the image through excellence of professional performance and faultless ethical behavior. Outstanding accomplishments in both spheres will materially aid the individual and simultaneously raise the prestige of the profession.

This discussion will therefore concern itself with the architect as social entity, his evolution and present public status. It will then treat the concepts of good and bad architects and finally deal with guidelines for coping with the complexities (and also perplexities) of codes of ethics.

The Architect's Characteristics

It is the architect who creates the framework of our physical environment, who, by proportioning space and materials, and by the subtle adjustments of nuances, molds and refines the substance of mankind's most conspicuous product, namely architecture. His abilities must encompass a vast range. He must be artist, engineer, and businessman.

His position in society should thus be clear; it is his noble task to partake in the shaping of culture. The architect's work assumes that significance through the advance creation of a structure. All activities henceforth taking place in it will be subject to the limits and influences of this very structure. The degree of its beauty, the elegance of its plan, its cost of operation — all will influence the functioning of the activities performed therein. For all this the architect is indeed responsible for he was the creator of that environment.

The Architect Then and Now

While the architect, by virtue of his knowledge and responsibility, should move about in lofty spheres, sundry circumstances have relegated him to a less exalted position. Has this great paradox between his responsibility and knowledge on one hand and his subordinate status on the other always existed? — the humiliating position in which he finds himself not infrequently, as he gets jostled about by the press, tossed through committees, bargained with as though he were a produce merchant.

No, in the past the architect was indeed the holder of lofty status. In antiquity he communicated mostly with those who held power: kings, generals and great political leaders. Ictinus, the architect of the Parthenon and (most probably) inventor of the Corinthian style, was a leading member of Pericles' own staff. The architects of the gigantic Ionic temples were constantly named together with the leaders of the time — Croesus, Alexander of Macedonia, and later the Emperors of Rome.

Relevant ancedotes, left by Vitruvius, give some idea of the architect's status in that society. His problem was quite similar to ours; to create beautifully and economically, and to communicate with the society. So dependent was society upon his superior ability that most drastic methods were used to assure his good performance. Vitruvius tells of a city of Hellenic Greece where the architect was required to pledge his personal estate as security against a possible excess in the cost of work. To exceed the budget by more than 25% was absolutely disastrous, but to remain within was equally well remunerated. Great public honors were bestowed upon him.

Vitruvius, through his celebrated treatise, most strongly influenced the professional position of architecture throughout the Roman, early Christian and even Middle Ages.

Later, about the time of the high Gothic, one meets other highly esteemed milestones of the profession — the works of men like Jean D'Orbais, the architect of Rheims, Robert de Luzarches of Amiens and Master Erwin of Strasbourg. Of course, as one approaches the more recent past, names and fame of architects were recorded with increasing accuracy. To whom are the names Bramante, Brunelleschi, Michelangelo and Bernini not familiar?

To these men, our architectural ancestors, we owe a debt greater than one can imagine: they have left the edifices which elevated architecture to the highest level of human accomplishment. Contemporary architects operate on the platform these men created.

The Break in the Pattern

With the exhaustion of styles, one notices the first signs of decay of architecture and with it the status of its masters. Almost simultaneously, the new technology, emerging from the industrial revolution, produced a new phenomenon — the engineer. His abilities were immediately recognized as very useful. He rapidly created new building materials and developed the art of reliable prediction of structural behavior. Inevitably, the engineer took over the segment of architecture which deals with technology. As a further decimation of the architect's realm, construction gradually came under the control of the general contractor. In the United States, architectural associations made the separation permanent through pragmatic renunciation of participation in construction.

And, after two and one-half millennia, the architect must deal with the first serious change in course. He has begun to call himself a professional, but with a considerable degree of uncertainty. The quantity of his knowledge is by no means less, neither are his responsibilities, but the decimation of his domain has not gone unnoticed by society.

The Public's Judgment

In the past, the public had to deal with the architect regardless, because he was also engineer and builder. Our society, being quite cognizant of the surrender of some of his authority to others, will now almost instinctively seek out the contractor for advice first. Furthermore, contractors, even engineers, are frequently used as checks and balance against the architect. His ability is questioned and doubted (in particular his cost estimates) and he is therefore often dependent upon the endorsement of the contracting trade.

The architect's last bastion is art. But the world of architecture with its indeterminate quantity of aesthetics is psychologically uncomfortable; the public resents what it does not understand. The very sober subjects of engineering and construction are now in the hands of someone else. The architect is left with the difficult defense of the artistic value. Aesthetics, previously accepted as part of the whole package, must now be taught to society singly. The teaching will require much time and effort.

The Architect's Status and His Conduct

While circumstances in our evolutionary pattern have placed us in a less desirable position than held by our predecessors, we architects seem to have within ourselves some very unfortunate features.

How can we hope to convince society that we still are the leaders in the world of building if our professional performance is not excellent, nor our integrity unquestionable? Success of one architect, for example, is belittled by his colleagues, if not openly envied. My colleague, my competitor – so do we see one another. We come to meetings with halos bigger than Doric capitals, speak loftily about the profession, the need for cooperative efforts. Yet when the client calls, we run for our personal profit. No longer are we professionals but avaricious businessmen. I should have had that job! The other man stole it from me! So we speak, self-righteously. This kind of conduct is well known to society. Should we then be surprised that we are not necessarily regarded as cultural leaders, which by vocation at least, we indeed are?

While society will tolerate business manners, the significant question remains: Is he a good or bad, great or small architect?

Let me define the bad architect first. Quite simply, his work is inferior – buildings ugly or uninspiring (a regression of culture), of unsound technical design (costly to maintain), or disorderly interior spaces (an obstacle to activity), or of high cost. While he may conceal his inabilities behind activities of a civic and philanthropic nature, he will never be regarded as a great architect.

The Good Architect

The good architect is, of course, the opposite. His work is good. His buildings have all the attributes of a lasting edifice. But the good architect is more. He is also that which he should be in the world of building – a leader not only in style and construction but in the very business of bringing a building into existence. The good architect does not wait until someone else discovers the necessity of a building. As the kingpin in the world of building, the good architect is precisely the one who determines the need for a new building.

I will admit that this, although the natural and correct process, is practically not easy to attain. But, the next best and attainable goal is the architect's leadership in the quest for the right building. A building adequate in size, suited for the purpose, of a design and plan possessing all the foresight possible, is the accomplishment of the great architect. Does a legislator know what kind of building is needed? Most certainly not! Yet he sits in judgment over something which was and still should be the architect's prerogative.

In my earlier years I was for some time attached to the staff of Arnold Steinbrecher, a great and noble Canadian architect of Russian descent. Arnold was in charge of the design of the Alberta Jubilee Auditoriums, two large concert halls built to commemorate the province's 50th anniversary. The project began under the auspices of the Department of Public Works, an institution which, by nature, is not expected to be the torch carrier of culture. As could be expected, the sum of ideas culminated in halls seating about 4,000 each, built of wood frame, to cost no more than 1.25 million dollars each. The legislature greedily grasped for these figures and proceeded with self-laudatory announcements of the coming world wonders to be erected at Edmonton and Calgary.

At about that point Arnold Steinbrecher was entrusted with the project. His first step was to make it clear to the Minister of the Department that one and a quarter million was not enough; that at least four and one half million per auditorium was needed. Next he undertook a difficult diplomatic campaign to tell the people in power that the program was wrong, that one does not build a good concert hall, let alone a legitimate theater, as large as 4,000 seating capacity — nor does one build of wood even if one is exempt from all codes. Steinbrecher gave speeches, produced figures, made proposals, researched data, pleaded and at times engaged in "collision" approaches with VIP's. After nearly four years of brilliant leadership, unselfish and exemplary behavior as architect, he succeeded in building Alberta's two great civic auditoriums. Ironically, the legislature requested that he place inscriptions on the buildings giving tribute to the pioneers of Alberta — and, if possible, including the government "unobtrusively." With his rare touch of humor, Steinbrecher instead quoted Suetonius: "He found the city built of brick, and left it built of marble."

Without Arnold Steinbrecher, the auditoriums would not exist as they do. This is the leadership I speak of.

The importance of truly professional behavior cannot be overstressed. If all architects exhibit greatness in knowledge and leadership, they will be highly regarded. The benefits are direct and immediate.

Ethics

Architects have, in most developed countries, established codes of ethics. The purpose is of course to give all members equal opportunity and encourage high moral standards, hoping thus to strengthen group and individual.

Yet the subject causes much internal confusion, anxiety and suspicion. Rather than relaxing under the safe shelter of the code of ethics, the architect becomes the strained interpreter of what he may or may not do, and finds himself in the role of the policeman of his colleagues. The demands for professional ethics, in particular on the smaller and newer firms, often seem unjust. Young architects are frequently bewildered by interpretation, usually in the spirit of Thrasymachus, who in Plato's *Republic* states: "Justice is the interest of the stronger."

Much of the confusion arises from the fact that the areas of the codes dealing with uniform behavior are not always logical, and those concerned with morals are utopian. Furthermore, the first group (free sketches, fees, etc.) is taken far too seriously and transgressions denounced profoundly, whereas the second (derogatory statements) is difficult to prove and therefore largely ignored. It reminds me of the police being able to catch speeders but not burglars.

The more technical rules of codes of ethics, like fee cutting, free sketches, competition, and advertising can be interpreted with relative ease. But the area of derogatory statements about one's colleagues cannot be controlled by a set of rules, because it is a moral matter resting in the character of a person. Transgressions in this area are very frequent. The damage done is immediate and often irreparable.

Competing Quite Generally

One cannot help but accept the premise of competition, even in the field of architecture. Not only do architects compete in quality and accomplishments, but also to stay in business. While they are competing for a project, they are businessmen and employ the standards of business: demonstration of ability, use of connections, glib talk, promises, and the cautious derogation of all competitors.

Let it be assumed that architects were to compete only on the basis of professional excellence. Neither connections nor business tactics would be allowed, only the elegance of the design, thoroughness of the construction documents and the meticulousness of supervision. Although the method would firstly benefit the owner, its deeper value would accrue to the professional community, for the competition would be on the basis of professionalism and abilities as artist and engineer.

It is therefore always in the interest of all concerned to promote most emphatically the idea of precisely administered competition. Competitions also stimulate great public curiosity and interest in the winner. Such open exposition of architecture is in the fullest interest of every architect.

Free Sketches

What exactly is a free sketch? The free sketch, which is considered a non-professional act, is an unsolicited drawing, usually of the exterior of the project the client intends to build. Architects who submit a sketch or rendering of the contemplated building do so for a number of reasons. When and under what circumstances is this method harmful to the profession?

First of all, there are several types of free sketches. There is the sketch made by the young architect who has no string of impressive buildings he could show to a prospective client. To him the sketch is a means to demonstrate his proficiency. Then there is the sketch which portrays an idea of a building. It could be compared perhaps to an invention or a musical composition. The architect with a new idea, whether he was commissioned for it or not, simply does what any artist is compelled to do: he renders his idea visible.

Then there is the sketch of the habitual free sketcher – the man who supplies the "come-on" rendering, mostly fake and as worthless as it is free. He caters only to that client who responds to loud advertising. Because his free sketch rarely has the attributes of good architecture, he is indeed harmful to the profession.

Let there be no mistake, in the competition for a project every competitor will, by law of nature, attempt to offer something other competitors cannot. If all architects would attempt to obtain the commission solely on the strength of their words, the best talker would be commissioned. If, on the other hand, they would appear with their firm's brochures and renderings of executed buildings, it is almost certain that he with the greatest quantity of material would walk away with the job. If, however, every architect would seek the commission by methods intrinsically his own, be it brochures, talk, free sketch, or the presentation of an idea, the owner would, in all probability, choose the man most suited for the project.

I should like to relate a personal experience which may show how differently free sketches are regarded by various people.

In the early days of my practice, one of my targets was to obtain bank work. I therefore concerned myself with the nature and design of branch banks. At the end of some fairly thorough studies I developed a design which was new, at least in the geographical area I worked in. I proceeded to put some ideas on paper and eventually presented these to the property management of one specific bank. I should also relate that much of the work of this bank was done by an old and well established firm. However, before I went to see the bank, I felt it necessary to reassure myself that my advance could not be classed as free sketches. I discussed the matter with several more experienced architects. The consensus of these men was that I had not produced a design for one particular building but more or less presented an idea, and for beginners the rule of free sketches is not fully applicable anyway. When I finally had the interview with the bank, I was shown, to my utter amazement, the rendering of a fairly futuristic and somewhat bizarre looking structure, a rendering which was authored by the old established architectural firm I just mentioned. It was explained to me that this design was supplied by that firm to "get us thinking" about a bank on a certain prominent piece of property. No more than a few days later I received a phone call from the senior partner of that architectural firm, criticizing me for having intruded on their realm! Eventually my design did lead to a small branch bank. The bizarre thing got built too, incidentally.

My advice to young architects who feel they must prepare designs to obtain commissions is that they do so in the best of professional taste. However, it is far more effective to illustrate an abstract idea than a particular building.

The Fee

Fortunately, the fee is left to the judgment of the individual architect. The only point codes of ethics make is that one should not reduce one's fee below that of one's competitor in order to obtain work. It must of course be presumed that the code considers all performances equal; i. e., for x percent fee, architects A, B, C and D will do precisely the same amount of work and of the same quality.

Nothing could be less true in practice. Not only are there vast differences in the quality of design, there are equally great differences in the perfection of construction and detailing, of the execution of contract documents, and of the quality of inspection. Not only that, but there are virtually no two buildings which require the same amount of work. Recommended sliding fee scales attempt to deal with the differences, but these attempts are not very realistic.

But let me return to the question of undercutting someone else's fee. First of all, it appears very hypothetical that one would know in advance what fees one's colleagues have asked for, unless one is openly told. Therefore, like all competing businessmen who must submit an offer, the architect is completely in the dark where he might stand in relation to his colleagues. Quite frankly, if another architect has offered to do a project for one-half percent less, one is not truly certain whether he has reduced his profit, or whether he intends to do that much less work. While it is up to each individual how much money he would like to make, it is of some concern to the professional community what the quality of his work should be since quality has something to do with the image of the profession.

The vagaries in all questions of fees and "fee cutting" are so great that it is almost idle to involve oneself in the question. I have found it to be fairest and clearest to all concerned to state the fee on an independent basis, to quote the amount I think I should receive because of the work involved and the quality standards of my organization.

Derogatory Statements

While the subjects just discussed are often grey areas where everybody will learn to be his own counsel, one must exercise the greatest conscientiousness, discipline and restraint when one gives witness about a fellow architect. While remaining entirely within the letter of the code, an architect can do immeasurable damage to another by making inappropriate statements. Can the reader perhaps recall a spell of momentary carelessness with his words? The writer certainly can!

It seems customary nowadays for a layman to ask one architect his opinion of another. Frequently, laymen will complain bitterly about something an architect has or has not done. The complaints are usually stated in a manner to invite concurring comment from the architect to whom the complaint was addressed. It is not always easy to avoid such situations. One may, with greatest care, comment, but it is wise to come to the defense of the colleague even if one does not really mean what one says.

On the other hand, if statements are volunteered, either carelessly or with the intent to lower the colleague's professional status, the architect is guilty of something like professional genocide. Nothing is more ruinous to the ethical image of the profession than such behavior and, of course, nothing is more harmful to the individual.

Like all hypocrisy, this form of misbehavior is quite elusive. I will therefore attempt to state in two examples what the architect under no circumstances should do.

Some years ago I received a commission for a country high school. Zealous young architect that I was, I delved into the problem with enthusiasm and came up with a fairly original shape for that time — a circular school with a system of expandable rings of classrooms around it. Members of the community received my proposal with different reactions — including indifference, enthusiasm and rejection. During various board meetings one private citizen made an undue amount of noise and finally admitted freely that she had an architect friend who told her that my design was not going to be inexpensive nor, in his opinion, very practical. Her vociferous and continued degradation of my professional status finally found sympathizers until my design had become untenable. Eventually, not only did the design have to be abandoned but the entire project. Much later I managed to learn through another colleague of the critical architect's reason for destructive intervention: in his opinion, he had to give truthful professional counsel to those who asked him! Although entirely within the code of ethics, it was completely unprofessional.

In another case, I had attempted for several years to obtain a commission in a large, continuing building project, in which one other architect had been primarily engaged. My attempts were soon noticed by the other architect. Quite naturally he resented me. Little, however, did I know that his resentment took the form of crafty derogatory statements not only directed to that client but also to other prospective clients. The day came when I obtained a commission and I hoped that the other architect would see the futility of his behavior. After I had completed my preliminary design, the other architect, with the expression of someone whose conscience can no longer be silent, remarked to our mutual client, "Rossman is going to have a problem with the drainage of that area." The remark triggered immediate deep concern in the client. My colleague fanned the matter into a real issue through continued discussion of "that unfortunate situation." It took many months and much work to regain the client's full confidence. The damage in this case was fortunately light.

In conclusion I would like to say that, by sheer logical deduction alone, it is an intrinsic feature of the effective architect to be fair and ethical. It is the perfect circle: he who conducts himself unethically is damaging someone else's livelihood. Since reprisals will be forthcoming, he cannot but see the value of following the guidelines of ethics.

chapter 14

The Coming Work
For Architects

ONE OF THE essentials of the effective architect is his continued awareness of the many kinds of structures needed to house the great multitude of activities of society. From this vast array of buildings he must choose for himself that segment for which he is best suited by personal inclination, professional training and practical experience.

This chapter therefore first reviews the many types and characteristics of buildings and who builds them. Subsequently it concerns itself with building growth pattern. Finally, methods to predict future patterns, as they will concern one's operation in the years hence, are discussed.

A Catalog of Building Types

In the subsequent categories, building types are arranged in the following order of importance:

    a) Purpose as related to human activity.
    b) Type of owner or controlling agency.

1. HOUSING: SINGLE-FAMILY HOMES
                               DUPLEXES, TRIPLEXES, SEMI-DETACHED HOUSES
                               APARTMENT BUILDINGS
                               DORMITORIES, LODGING HOUSES

ARCHITECTURE:

Being largest in volume, the field is very competitive. The architect must make a continual surveillance of living habits, customs, new materials and fixtures, etc. New ideas are constantly demanded. Technically the field is quite uncomplicated.

OWNER:

Predominantly private except dormitories, which are usually public.

2. PUBLIC EDUCATION: ELEMENTARY AND HIGH SCHOOLS
                                    JUNIOR, TECHNICAL AND BUSINESS COLLEGES
                                    UNIVERSITIES
                                    MUSIC SCHOOLS
                                    LIBRARIES, MUSEUMS

ARCHITECTURE:

The entire field is interesting and challenging. While it is quite competitive, the architect with new ideas, together with a thorough grounding in the process of learning at all levels and an understanding of how to display accumulated knowledge, will be very successful.

OWNER:

Both public and private.

3. RELIGION: CHURCHES
                               SYNAGOGUES
                               COMMUNITY HALLS
                               CONVENTS, MONASTERIES
                               SEMINARIES

ARCHITECTURE:

The field is very fascinating and requires a high degree of special knowledge and experience. Essential are complete familiarity with church building history and personal acquaintance with all major historical religious buildings. More than any other kind of building, churches require utmost discipline and taste in design.

As a note of reflection I would like to add that the church architect must be able to sustain disappointments.

OWNER:

Private, generally representing large groups of people. Subject to committee control.

4. PUBLIC ENTERTAINMENT: CONCERT HALLS
                              OPERA HOUSES
                              LEGITIMATE THEATERS
                              OPEN-AIR THEATERS
                              MOTION PICTURE HOUSES

ARCHITECTURE:

This segment in the world of building demands some high technical specialization, plus good background in drama and music. Excepting motion picture theaters, experience is usually gained very slowly due to the rarity of such structures.

The segment is one of the few glamour areas of architecture. Fame or humiliation seem the only possible outcomes.

OWNER:

Usually public. Smaller establishments privately owned.

5. PUBLIC AMUSEMENT: ARENAS
                          STADIA AND GRANDSTANDS
                          EXHIBITION BUILDINGS
                          AMUSEMENT PARK STRUCTURES
                          RECREATION PIERS
                          BOWLING ALLEYS
                          SWIMMING POOLS
                          SKATING RINKS

ARCHITECTURE:

Arenas, stadia and exhibition buildings are usually so large they are more structure than architecture. Not a very high level of specialization is needed. Experience can be gathered by studying existing buildings. The remaining types are simple large halls in which recreational equipment of one kind or another is housed.

OWNER:

Both public and private. Since governments are not in the business of "entertaining," arenas, stadia, etc., are managed by government-controlled private groups.

6. PUBLIC HEALTH AND WELFARE: HOSPITALS AND CLINICS
                                   INFIRMARIES
                                   SANATORIUMS
                                   NURSING, CONVALESCENT AND
                                     REST HOMES
                                   MENTAL HOSPITALS
                                   NURSERIES
                                   ORPHANAGES
                                   OLD AGE HOMES

ARCHITECTURE:

Here indeed is a field complex enough to warrant almost exclusive specialization. Multitudinous are the disorders of mind, body and social behavior; so must be the means and facilities to cure them.

OWNER:

Usually private and subject to committees.

7. PUBLIC SAFETY: POLICE STATIONS
                        COURT HOUSES
                        JAILS, PRISONS
                        REFORMATORIES
                        FIRE STATIONS

ARCHITECTURE:

This variety is of medium complexity. Most owners prescribe all major features — the architect is more the overall planner. While not the most cheerful of building types, it is one in which the designing architect must concentrate on the humanitarian aspect. Buildings of this nature are not infrequent.

OWNER:

Wholly governmental.

8. NATIONAL DEFENSE: ACADEMIES
                           OFFICES
                           HOUSING
                           HOSPITALS, CHAPELS
                           RESEARCH FACILITIES
                           SHOPS
                           HANGARS
                           BARRACKS, STORES, ARMORIES

ARCHITECTURE:

Technically, most structures for the armed forces fall into one or another category. Therefore, whatever specialization is required, is applicable for any given building. The administrative portion of a project, also known as red tape, approaches that of the technical. The architect must be prepared to live and work by the book.

OWNER:

Owners are state and federal governments.

9. GOVERNMENT: ADMINISTRATIVE AND LEGISLATIVE STRUCTURES
                     POST OFFICES
                     AIR TRAFFIC CONTROL AND METEOROLOGY

> RESEARCH LABORATORIES
> MATERIALS CONTROL LABORATORIES
> INDIAN FACILITIES
> MONUMENTS
> HIGHWAY DEPOTS

ARCHITECTURE:

Government buildings, as can be seen from the above list, come in a great variety. Special knowledge is required for several types. The category is interesting and worthwhile.

OWNER:

Government-controlled agencies.

10. PUBLIC TRANSPORTATION: AIRPORT TERMINALS
FREIGHT AND AIRCRAFT MAINTENANCE
RAILWAY STATIONS
BUS STATIONS
HARBORS, DOCKS, HARBOR TERMINALS

ARCHITECTURE:

Due to the highly technical nature of transportation, the architectural requirements are, of course, quite special. This applies in particular to air travel, which presently surpasses all other building developments in continued progress and change.

It is very advisable to have a solid grounding in general mechanical engineering before one plans to become active in the field of public transportation architecture.

OWNER:

Authorities, governments and private concerns.

11. INDUSTRIAL: GENERAL MANUFACTURING PLANTS
FOUNDRIES
CHEMICAL PLANTS
ELECTRONICS PLANTS
RESEARCH PLANTS
TEXTILE MILLS
MINING AND SMELTING
FOOD PRODUCTION, CREAMERIES, DAIRIES
FOOD STORAGE PLANTS, REFRIGERATION PLANTS
WORKSHOPS AND PRINTING PLANTS
TELEPHONE BUILDINGS
POWER PLANTS
BREWERIES AND DISTILLERIES
REFINERIES

ARCHITECTURE:

The architectural requirements in industry are strictly subordinated to the technological purpose of a given building. Specialization, therefore, is essential. Again a good background in engineering is the first prerequisite to success in industrial architecture.

OWNER:

Private concerns.

12. BUSINESS: OFFICES, FOR ALL BUSINESSES AND
                PROFESSIONAL ACTIVITIES
                PARKING GARAGES

ARCHITECTURE:

This field, centering around the multi-story office building, is highly competitive. Architecturally, it is one of the simplest. Any architect with the least amount of research and specialization can enter the field.

Parking garages are a specialty, but wide open for the new idea.

OWNER:

Business owners are all private.

13. SALES: DEPARTMENT STORES
            RETAIL STORES AND SHOPS
            MERCANTILE ESTABLISHMENTS
            SALES ROOMS
            WHOLESALE HOUSES
            PRINTING SHOPS
            GAS STATIONS
            CAR AGENCIES
            MANUFACTURERS' OUTLETS

ARCHITECTURE:

In the vast field of merchandising, a certain degree of specialization is essential. Originality and appeal are the key notes.

OWNER:

Private.

14. PERSONAL SERVICE: MEDICAL AND DENTAL OFFICES
                        PROFESSIONAL OFFICES – DOCTORS,
                          LAWYERS, ARCHITECTS, ENGINEERS,
                          SURVEYORS
                        RESTAURANTS, NIGHT CLUBS
                        HOTELS
                        BARBER AND BEAUTY SHOPS

FUNERAL HOMES
DRYCLEANING PLANTS
... AND MANY OTHERS

ARCHITECTURE:

Quite generally there is functional specialization in most of these building types. In particular, restaurants, night clubs, and hotels require not only special knowledge but also a special flair in designing for elegance and the appearance of luxury.

OWNER:

With very few exceptions, private.

15. SEMI-PUBLIC ENTERTAINMENT: CLUB HOUSES
GOLF, YACHT, SKIING, TENNIS
MIXED ACTIVITY

ARCHITECTURE:

Club house architecture is a class of its own. It can best be defined as a place for adults to play.

OWNER:

Private groups ranging from 50 to 500, committee controlled.

16. NEWS AND BROADCASTING: RADIO BROADCASTING STUDIOS
MOTION PICTURE STUDIOS
TELEVISION STUDIOS
BROADCASTING STUDIOS
NEWSPAPER OFFICES AND PRINT ROOMS

ARCHITECTURE:

Radio, TV and motion picture broadcasting studios are in essence uncomplicated, large halls, with special acoustic requirements. These types of buildings are best suited for the more technical architect.

OWNER:

Private concerns.

17. AGRICULTURE: SILOS, GRAIN ELEVATORS
FEED MILLS
STORAGE SHEDS
REFRIGERATED STORAGE PLANTS
COTTON GINS

ARCHITECTURE:

Architecture is exclusively industrial and can be quite challenging. While this field is not an obvious one, it is nevertheless fairly large.

OWNER:

Private or cooperative.

18. SCIENTIFIC STRUCTURES: ASTRONOMICAL OBSERVATORIES
    METEOROLOGICAL STATIONS
    AQUARIUMS
    ATOMIC ACCELERATOR STATIONS
    SPACE PROGRAM BUILDINGS
    TRACKING STATIONS

ARCHITECTURE:

Extremely specialized and highly fascinating. Due to rarity, only a handful of architects will ever come in touch with these buildings. Anyone aspiring to work in this field should be prepared for several years of special study, participation in scientific colloquiums, and publication of papers.

OWNER:

Usually governmental.

Self-Analysis of Activities

The reader who has reviewed this catalog will be compelled to re-evaluate his organization so that two crucial questions may be answered:

A. Are there fields in which one is not engaged, but has special abilities? Could new fields of work be entered into?

B. How are one's activities distributed? Is one's organization utilizing special capabilities concentrating on like types? Or is there a wide, perhaps aimless, scattering, suggesting abandonment of certain fields?

Entering New Fields of Work

Potential new fields of work exist wherever building types, regardless of category, are congruent in function, architecture and structure. The architect who masters a type in one category is well prepared to master similar types in other categories. For example, an architect experienced in restaurants or night clubs is well qualified to design country clubs, motels, dance halls and amusement park structures. Or, if one's training lies in the area of hospitals, one will do well in the design of most laboratories, doctors' offices, or even pharmaceutical industries. Again, similarity of experience is required for the design of large manufacturing halls, airplane hangars, storage buildings and even exhibition halls. A study of the preceding catalog will reveal many fields of similarity.

Abandonment of Weak Fields

If, on the other hand, the analysis shows a wide scattering of activity, it is usually wise to consider what a clean consolidation could do for one's business. Scattering has the serious drawback one meets in virtually every field — the competition of the specialist. For example, if I have only superficial experience in hospitals, and apply for a commission of a large hospital in competition with a firm highly specialized in this field, my chances are indeed small.

Preparing for the Future

As can be seen in the foregoing, a significant step toward a more efficient operation is the re-evaluation of one's capabilities and special strengths.

To fully establish one's participation in the world of building, it is necessary to develop a knowledge of trends of the future. To do so, three steps are necessary. First, one must study and anticipate the future course of building. Secondly, one must choose the direction in which one plans to go. Thirdly, one must prepare to function efficiently in the years hence. I shall speak extensively about the third step in chapter 15.

Anticipating the Future

Encouragingly, the future will bring an ever increasing volume of construction. The prime causes are the inevitable increase in population and the increase in wealth quite generally.

In the wake of population expansion follows the demand for more and more construction. The rise in wealth adds larger space needs, more luxury and elaborate appointments. Fig. 14.1 shows the relationships between anticipated population expansion and increase in construction. Fig. 14.2 illustrates the distribution of the major fields of construction.

In the 18-year period 1950 to 1968 population increased by 25% and is expected to increase by 36% in the seventeen-year period 1968 to 1985. Construction volume per year better than doubled in those 18 years. Following closely the pattern of population increase, construction can be expected nearly to double its 1968 volume by 1985. This means that the average architectural office could expect an increase in work volume of almost 6% per year.

In the broad outlines of the major fields of construction, we recognize the primary significance of residential building. While it is quantitatively the largest segment, commerce and industry have shown spectacular increases, better than doubling their volume in the past 20 years. The same applies to public education.

As illustrated in Figure 14.2, certain shifts of emphasis are evident. These shifts are due to changing habits of our society.

In the past twenty-five years the number of people who have decided that metropolitan living is more desirable than owning private homes or farms has increased by 10%. This has caused a considerable growth of apartment buildings, and quite generally re-urbanization of previously stagnant city areas. The trend toward urbanization parallels the rise of personal income over the same period. It can be safely predicted that there will be further urbanization and construction of the necessary structures.

Because of the great trend toward a levelled society, construction has experienced a

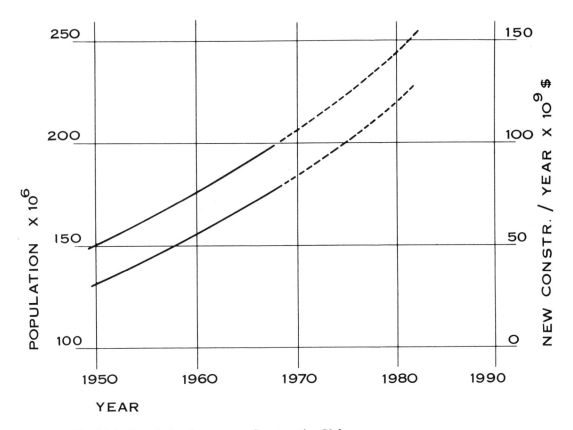

Fig. 14.1 Population Increase vs. Construction Volume

shift toward public buildings, primarily in welfare and education. It appears certain that this trend will continue, bringing yet greater increases in public structures.

To name a less obvious shift, the decrease of working hours per week has resulted in an increase of leisure time, requiring more recreational structures such as private clubs, resorts, hotels, national park facilities. Religious buildings, on the other hand, have experienced very little increase because of our decreasing interest in worship.

Other fluctuations are more sporadic. For example, many of our city centers experience their first major rebuilding, causing a spectacular advance in the development of civic structures.

Fluctuations also occur through mass migration into new and more promising geographical areas. Our society is becoming less and less rooted or locality bound. These migrations will continue. Anyone seeking virgin territory for construction might cast an eye upon the geographical areas of small population but large natural resources.

Changes in the political milieu can alter the pattern. For example, localities receiving sudden large governmental appropriations for projects such as space flight, will experience sudden progress. Conversely, an area may become depressed due to abandonment of industries out of political expediency. And, in a depressed area, the architect is among the first to suffer.

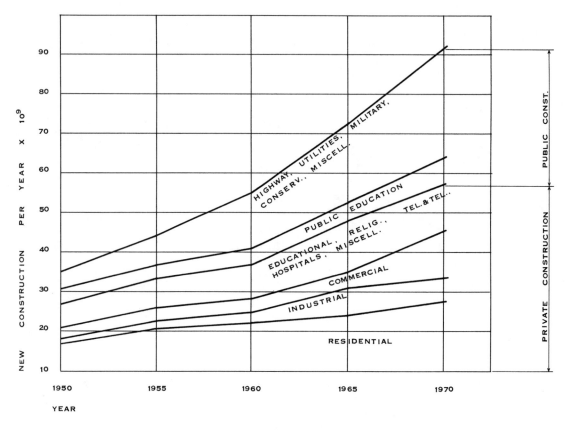

Fig. 14.2 Construction Volume in the Major Fields

Our technology also causes continued changes. Speaking only of transportation, the private automobile has changed our cities most profoundly in the last few decades. Aviation will do the same in the future. In consequence, many new types of structures will be invented and built, analogous to the parking garage which was a newcomer once.

To arrive at a meaningful interpretation of all this, as it might affect one's organization, one must investigate the future course of construction in one's immediate geographical area. The data needed is usually available from local or federal governmental agencies (such as the U.S. Department of Commerce). The following method will give a reasonably sensible picture:

    a) Determine the pattern of population expansion
    b) The construction pattern of at least the following fields should be studied:
        1) Housing
        2) Public Buildings
        3) Commercial
        4) Industrial

Housing is the most significant indicator of the future growth pattern.

Public buildings indicate the sociological environment. A society tending to social equality will create more institutional buildings.

Commerce and industry, because of their respective interdependence, are self-regenerating. Areas showing great increases in commercial activities will experience accelerated growth in that particular field. The same holds true for industry.

While more detailed research is, of course, desirable, the information gained from this study gives a general pattern of past building activities. Employing the method of reasoning outlined previously, the architect can make intelligent predictions of future building activities for his immediate area.

Charting the Course

Once probable future construction has been revealed, the architect must consider his organization's opportunities of sharing in the coming activities. Evidence of a definite trend should entice the architect to consider the potential, and align his capabilities with the coming demands. Should he already be in the predictable mainstream, he ought to redouble his efforts for excellence of performance, lest he be overtaken.

I have found it most useful to take at least one day every year to conduct a study of these trends and movements which will affect my business. It has enabled me to pattern much of my research and preparatory activities towards those fields in which I might be engaged profitably some day. Also important is the periodic review of all fields an architect might enter. It is this periodic self-analysis which determines the major course in which the architect must pilot his own enterprise.

chapter 15

The Architect's Education
After School

To PRACTICE EFFECTIVELY, the architect must unceasingly further his knowledge through systematic self-education. He must develop his critical judgment and good taste to design not only more perfectly but also faster and more efficiently. An unerring ability to create environments which will be experienced exactly as he desired must be one of his ultimate goals. Upon this ability rests the mastery of architecture.

This chapter deals with the analysis of one's knowledge, the formulation of study plans, the choice of texts and methods of study. It concludes with the aspects of travel study, recommendations of edifices to be visited and some pointers of what to look for.

The Avenues to Education

The universities are becoming more and more the place where the basics of the profession of architecture are being taught. Most schools offer curricula with increasing emphasis on design and have added semesters to cope with the ever greater demands for more and broader knowledge in the practice of the profession. Yet, as practicing architects know, and new graduates learn in a succession of sometimes rude shocks, the system has not produced an immediately usable professional personage. In fact it rarely yields more than a beginning draftsman. Discouragingly, the area in which training was most thorough, namely design, is the one in which the new graduate is least trusted. No architect is wild about having a new graduate on the staff; if he has a disproportionate number in his employ, his practice may suffer seriously. The cause for this situation is the one-sidedness of the curricula which emphasize a kind of unbridled design fervor at the expense of a disciplined system of practice and study. Admittedly the range of new ideas is sometimes quite spectacular, but the number of useful solutions is very small.

In practical life the pattern manifests itself in the profusion of aimless designs put forth by the professional army in juxtaposition to the limited quantity of excellent creations by the gifted few.

While there is no substitute for originality, good architecture is still the product of an architect skilled in the art of design. The skill can be attained through disciplined study and practice. Because the now generally offered curricula lack these fundamentals, practicing architects must acquire them in a process of well planned self-study. Once an architect has attained the ability critically to judge his work, his buildings will exhibit greater maturity and usefulness, and his approach to design be much more efficient.

The now almost extinct technical college produced the more practical-minded architect. Emphasis was placed on drafting, building construction, some simple statics and equipment engineering. At times, crafts typical in the building industry were also taught and students reached a surprising degree of proficiency. While the graduate was almost immediately useful in the professional community, he rarely progressed beyond a certain level above which more theoretical and specific knowledge is necessary. His greatest lack was knowledge of architectural history, the essence of art in architecture, design and, to some extent, fundamentals of more complex statics. This lack he must now remedy through ardent study of historic structures, both practical and theoretical, as well as of the elements of statics.

Quite frequently the architect is one who has advanced from draftsman. While outdistancing university and college graduates in drafting and very often construction detailing, his knowledge is usually fragmentary, lacking theory and design abilities. Meeting registration requirements makes his knowledge more coherent but does not give him the depth for mature designs. To elevate his knowledge to the level of his colleagues, studies must be in fields similar to those mastered by the technical college graduate. Apart from that, lack of education in humanities is often evident. And architecture as one of the pillars of culture is unthinkable without philosophic foundations.

The master's apprentice ranks highest in possession of intrinsic architectural knowledge. From the beginning of his studies he is exposed to the taste, critical judgment, culture and tone of the master. He receives knowledge not laterally but omni-directionally. Virtually no facet of architectural education is slighted. His education never ceases — it will continue with the instilled momentum. Perhaps the only danger is the acquisition of a narrowness of viewpoint, suppressing originality through unquestioned acceptance of everything the master has taught. The master's apprentice should polish his taste primarily by travel study and the reading of philosophers.

The Study Plan

As the foregoing has shown, no architect is without voids in his professional knowledge. To determine these voids, it usually suffices to reach for a text about any of the major fields — history, structure, building materials, professional practice — and by random sampling compare one's memory to established knowledge.

Little needs to be said about the technical and business phases. The degree and areas of lack of knowledge soon become evident and will call for remedial studies, following suitable texts.

As discussed previously, lack of knowledge of historic structure is usually more common and also a greater detriment. One must bear in mind that nearly all phases of architecture — engineering, business, etc. — can be, and often are, taken care of by non-architects. Design, however, is intrinsically the architect's prerogative. His abilities must therefore be greatest here, and architectural history is fundamental. Therefore, all architectural study-plans will inevitably center around this subject. The study-plan should contain the twofold approach of theoretical study and practical visits.

The theoretical study must concern itself with architectural history and more specifically, the underlying causes and reasons for historic structures, the thought behind them. One should be conversant with texts covering the classic periods, such as Vitruvius, Robertson, Berve and Gruben. Next, at least a pictorial study of early Christian and Romanesque structures is advisable. Gothic should be studied and comprehended in as much depth as possible. Here the incomparable texts of Hans Jantzen are most lucid. Apart from the study of texts, it is most rewarding to sketch the significant features of an entire structure and also details. For example, to draw side by side one window bay of Amiens, Chartres, Rheims and Beauvais respectively (Fig. 15.1) is exceedingly interesting since it teaches such concepts as theme and its variations in near perfect succession, a concept applicable for most design work in one's office.

The extent of thought given to planning, situating, and, of course, proportioning classic temples is always refreshing and stimulating. Proportions are treated most thoroughly by Vitruvius and Palladio.

Travel Study

The combination of theoretical and travel study teaches two fundamentals of the architect's work: the abstract concept on paper and its extension into tangible reality of space, light and boundaries.

Few architects have the ability to assess a design for its psychological impact upon the user. What proportions, colors, surface features, spatial arrangements, light and acoustics stimulate what feelings, reactions? The way to achieve mastery of these design parameters is first to experience many kinds of environments. This can only be accomplished through visits to significant buildings and inquiry into their nature. At one time a personal visit to the major historical buildings was essential for the architect's education. Today the necessity is even greater; the almost limitless range of possibilities with modern materials demands greater discipline of use.

Therefore travel study must be the first and most important item in the study-plan of the practicing architect.

To make it a profitable venture, it should be planned and undertaken in small but thorough steps. For example, an architect may take the Greek classic first. Essential then is the thorough study of those structures one plans to see. These structures should be studied so well in advance that, upon visiting them, one immediately feels at home.

Leaving all camera gear behind, the visits must be systematic — beginning with a slow approach on foot, next a deliberate touring of the building and then, if possible, a circumnavigation. Thus one obtains an overall picture. Then comes the detailed visit. To let the environment speak, whenever possible, periods of contemplation of at least fifteen minutes should be inserted. Very important is the observation of the changing day from dawn to sunset, the play of light and the apparent variations of proportions. Useful is a mental measure of height of a room, its breadth, its length, the subordinate and decorative details and their scale. Since materials and surfaces play an important role, it is often significant to touch the stone or wood — the reality assumes a new dimension thus. When I first visited the Apollo temple at Didyma, I was fascinated to find that the marble stones of the walls, although 2,300 years old, felt like velvet.

Finally, he who visits the Greek temples in particular will be delirious about the perfection of workmanship, so heart-warming to the modern American architect in his daily battles for good quality in construction.

A further step in the broadening of the architect's knowledge lies in participation in colloquiums and conventions. Such participation sharpens one's cognizance of contemporary thought, and greatly aids in evaluation of one's position in the competitive professional society. The extent of one's knowledge of current structures, new thoughts and behavioral patterns of our society can thus be evaluated and where necessary amended.

Objects of Study Travel

The prime purpose of study travel is to discover the thing that made these buildings timelessly admired and beautiful, to discover that substance, so one may apply the discovered thoughts to one's own designs. Listed below are those architectural edifices which are, in the opinion of the author, among the most outstanding examples of the respective styles and periods.

Greek Classic

Greece:	Acropolis (Athens)
	Cape Sunium
	Delphi
	Apheae (Isle of Aegina)
Turkey:	Priene
	Miletus
	Ephesus
	Didyma

CHARTRES 1194 **AMIENS 1220**

Fig. 15.1 Theme and variation in the high Gothic. All forms are true to the rules,
the theme. The artistry lies in the proportioning of the theme and variation of detail.

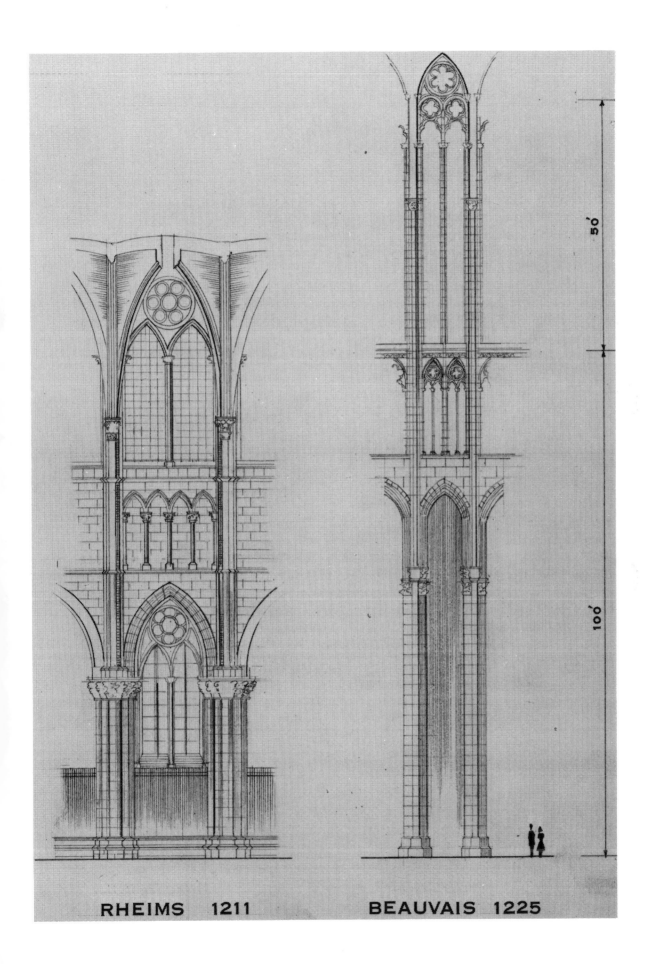

RHEIMS   1211   **BEAUVAIS   1225**

50'

100'

Sicily:	Agrigento
	Selinus
Italy:	Paestum

The features most important to observe are the use of one material throughout, design, proportion and exquisite workmanship. Of particular interest is the Propylaea at the Acropolis of Athens. Because of the beautiful solution of a very difficult design problem, I have often considered the Propylaea a spectacular example for the practicing contemporary architect. Of considerable interest, in particular for their masterplanning, are Delphi, Priene and Miletus. No one has presented in greater depth and more interesting vernacular the fascinating developments of these cities than Berve and Gruben. These edifices should not be visited without preceding study of their text or another suitable one.

Roman Classic

Rome:	Forum, Colosseum
	Pantheon
	Thermae
	Basilica of Maxentius
France:	Nimes, Maison Carée
	Orange, Theater
	Pont du Gard

Roman structures at the Forum and perhaps the Thermae of Caracalla are foremost in the representation of the arch. One is always deeply impressed by their boldness and size. While almost completely lacking the finesse of the Greek temples, the Roman buildings exhibit engineering spirit, manifested magnificently in the Pont du Gard. The visiting architect should observe the inventiveness of design with few simple media: stone or brick and arch or vault. Most strongly recommended is the sketching of the arches of Septimus Severus and Titus, down to small detail.

Byzantine

Turkey:	Hagia Sophia (Istanbul)
	Church of Irene (Istanbul)
	(Several of the famous mosques of more recent vintage such as the Sultan Ahmet I [Blue Mosque] and Sultan Suleiman at Istanbul)
Italy:	San Marco (Venice)
	San Vitale (Ravenna)

One of the most worthwhile things to discover in Byzantine structures is the spatial magnificence and color of surface treatment. In this particular regard, Sultan Ahmet leaves one breathless, whereas the Hagia Sophia must still await complete restoration before the opaque veil of age is lifted. Deeply impressive are also such structures as the great mosque at Bursa (Turkey), or the little church of Daphne outside of Athens. Both give one the feeling of having left the world behind, as though one were permitted to experience the ante-room of His Kingdom.

Early Christian

Italy: Santa Maria Maggiore (Rome)
San Paolo Fuori Le Mura (Rome)
Santa Sabine (Rome)

One would be guilty of gross negligence not to visit at least St. Maria Maggiore and San Paolo while at Rome. The outstanding characteristics of these early Christian churches is the irrepressible desire they give the visitor to lift his gaze again and again to the magnificence of the coffered ceilings of gold and color. If one should ever wish to learn to what perfection the design of a ceiling can be carried, one must see the early Christian churches in Rome.

Romanesque

Italy: Asti
San Zeno (Verona)

France: St. Gilles (Arles)

Germany: Limburg

Within the great structures of the Romanesque time, almost devoid of ornamentation, only stone verticals, vaults and arches create the space, a space penetrated by narrow shafts of light. These buildings again cause an entirely different feeling in the viewer. Most useful in the study of extreme asceticism is the employment of effects and materials. It should be observed that the Italian Romanesque is the most playful, the French the grandest in design and concept, and the German farthest advanced. Most worthwhile is a visit to Limburg which, similar to Aix-la-Chapelle (Aachen) and San Vitale, has the amazing height to width relation, almost forcing the mind to think and feel in vertical terms only.

Gothic

France: Rheims
Chartres
Amiens
Notre Dame of Paris
Strasbourg

Germany: Cologne

England: Lincoln
Exeter

Italy: Santa Croce
             Milan
             Siena
             Orvieto

While all other styles could be ignored, the Gothic rarely leaves a mind untouched. He who has experienced in their entirety such cathedrals as Chartres or Strasbourg will never be able to banish from his mind a permanent impression. When only limited time is available, I have found the cathedrals of the high Gothic in northern France deserving a visit before anything else. Ideally, no cathedral should receive less attention than a full day's visit in order to comprehend its spatial effects, its religious influence and omnipresence in the community. Any serious student discovers with amazement that the cathedral is not an integral part of the town, but the town an integral part of the cathedral. Among the points of particular interest, at least to the author, have been the west work of Strasbourg, the deep warmth of Chartres with its almost unearthly blue and purple light, the design of the three rose windows at Amiens and the nearly complete unification of religion and architecture of Rheims. Each building is too vast to be sketched in any detail. It is advisable to descend for example upon one window and draw its proportions and details to great accuracy. Finally, no architect should ignore the sculptures in any one of these cathedrals.

Renaissance

Italy: Palazzi Pitti & Strozzi (Florence)
             Capitol (Rome)
             Vatican (Rome)
             Santa Susanna (Rome)
             Lateran (Rome)
Germany: Andechs
             Wies
             St. Michaels (Munich)

France:
Austria: Royal Palaces
England:

While visiting these structures one becomes particularly conscious of the ornateness of the Renaissance. Because it is an architecture which lends itself to grandeur, in particular the larger complexes like the great royal palaces of central Europe and England, it teaches much about overall planning arrangements (and the almost limitless application of ornaments). Somewhat separate are the baroque churches of Bavaria which demonstrate baroque to be a surface characteristic equally beautiful in the Gothic hall-church of Andechs, as in the more Romanesque forms of a church like Rottenbuch or the pure baroque of Wies.

The traveling architect must, of course, keep his eyes open and look at any building exhibiting outstanding characteristics. This holds true for historic and contemporary structures. The architect must train his mind to recognize timeless features of beauty (also those of cheap mannerism) and eventually design according to his well-developed judgment.

The modern world is accustomed to learn by viewing film strips and video tapes. Life itself, however, is the grandest of all film strips and nothing can teach the open-minded person faster and more profoundly.

Fig. 15.2 Apollo Temple of Didyma (Southwest Turkey). Like few other antique structures, the Didymaeum has a plan of mathematical clarity. Walls and stylobate possess convex curvatures. Wall stone blocks are therefore parallelograms. All details are carried out with inevitable consistency, never violating self-imposed law. The temple is very large (columns about 64 feet high).

Fig. 15.3 Cape Sunium, Poseidon Temple. The significance of the Poseidon temple to the visiting architect is a kind of maximum effect with minimum effort. White marble against the blue Mediterranean sky! The rhythmic arrangement of slender doric columns, an entablature (only indicative now) and remnants of a stylobate. How many applications does this constellation of one material, three elements and air have in modern buildings?

Fig. 15.4 Erechtheum (Acropolis, Athens). A spectacular array of design solutions meets the visitor to the Erechtheum. Through considerable changes of levels, with a constant variation of proportions a theme is retained. Complicated details are solved with ease and elegance. Somewhat like the Propylaea, a variety of functions placed great limitations on the design. Obviously, rather than submitting to weariness, the designing architects resolved the problems with superb diligence.

Fig. 15.5 Pont du Gard (Provence, France). How would a modern architect solve this problem: an aqueduct about 880 feet long, crossing a valley 156 feet deep, also providing an economic roadway, to be built of hewn stone and weak mortar, no mathematics, no testing labs? The point of significance: a design of inexorable logic resulting in both economy and beauty.

Fig. 15.6   Portal, St. Gilles (Provence, France). I have often wondered by what path of thought the architect of St. Gilles arrived at a design of such contrast: the richly sculptured portals set into an almost featureless rectangle of stone, rising from a straight multistep stylobate. The effect is amazing since it projects the silvery overtones of an alleluia into the matrix of Romanesque somberness. A thought to study, a building to experience!

Fig. 15.7 Mosque Sultan Ahmet I (Istanbul). Relatively new (about 1600), this Mosque is modeled after the Hagia Sofia and therefore Byzantine in its features. As with all Byzantine churches and mosques, one experiences the feeling of awe in the vastness of Sultan Ahmet. Most remarkable are the colors of blue in the cladding tile work, contrasting with the multi-layered red carpets. Sultan Ahmet provides one of the paramount study subjects of color, space and surface treatment to the modern architect.

Fig. 15.8 Strasbourg Cathedral (France). A description giving this building justice would fill pages! Nevertheless, note that all circles melt into unity at points of tangency; note also the great themes of square, circle, steeple and pointed arches, the perfect harmony of the rosewindow tracery, the proportions of its members. To comprehend the cultural significance of Strasbourg, I recommend the reading of Goethe's famous letter written to D. M. Ervini A Steinbach, the master of Strasbourg, 450 years after Erwin's death. Who of our contemporary architects might leave a second Strasbourg to the world?

Fig. 15.9 Rheims Cathedral (France). "Ecclesia materialis significat ecclesiam spiritualem." "The material church signifies the spiritual church." Thus, the church becomes an architectural statement of contemporary spirit of faith and inclination to God. Nowhere, therefore, does the architect's work assume more transcendental significance than in the design of churches, and nowhere is the study of those who have preceded us in suffering and accomplishment more rewarding. Rheims is a symphony in architecture, an organpoint supporting jubilating choirs of light, verticals, sculptures, theologic implication, colors of all moods and, above all, the feeling of Sursum Corda.

Index